GROW RICH WITH
REAL ESTATE

GROW RICH WITH REAL ESTATE

My personal stories and advice for successful real estate investing

Written by Kevin Erwin
Edited by Cheryl LePlatt

ISBN: 1518739245
ISBN 13: 9781518739248

Foreword

This is a book about my adventures with real estate and business, many examples of success and some of failure. This book contains my thoughts and personal opinions on what it takes to be successful. Included are several personal experiences in business and real estate.

I hope this book will help you on your journey to success as you build confidence in the fact that anyone can be successful if he or she has passion and determination. My personal experiences can help you avoid the pitfalls on your journey.

"You can have anything you want if you want it badly enough. You can be any-thing you want to be, do anything you set out to accomplish if you hold to that desire with singleness of purpose."

ABRAHAM LINCOLN

How to become wealthy

Most people think becoming wealthy means getting a good education and then finding a good job. The fact is that few wealthy people actually have a job. I am not saying they do not work. The wealthy work for themselves; they do not work for somebody else. The wealthy normally work harder than people with jobs. The idea of working 40 hours per week is not in the successful business owner's vocabulary. The successful do whatever it takes. The slogan I told myself over and over again when I started my Allstate business was **"Failure is not an option"**. There are no magical words or specific things that I can say to you to make you become successful. If it were easy to be successful or make a lot of money, everyone would do it.

As you read through my stories, you will realize that the one characteristic I seem to repeat is the ability to take action on a project or business. I am not the smartest person in the room but probably above average since I took action and earned a master's degree in Finance. The taking action part also entails a calculated risk. To be successful you will need to evaluate the situation and determine if the potential gain or profit outweighs the potential risk.

Are you the type of person who will be able to make the hard decisions to push forward and take action? Well, are you? There will always be some risk to taking action.

The goal should be to own as many assets as you can. Assets are what generate income and create your cash flow.

Assets can include many different things. The most common types of assets include businesses, properties, or royalties. A business, property, or royalty can potentially create unlimited revenue for the owner. This book will talk about some of the assets I have acquired. These include commercial rentals, residential rentals, businesses, billboards, stock ownership and storage containers.

When someone states that another person is wealthy, I chuckle and always ask, "How do you know?"

The response is usually something like, because the other person makes $150,000 per year. Remember, financial wealth is not what you earn; financial wealth is the value of the assets you currently own.

The first commercial property I purchased is called Colonial Park. See picture below.

This is a 6900 square foot office building that sits on a main road in a growing area. This property has the general layout that I like. The units are 500-1200 square feet and are easily accessible. There are two identical buildings facing each other. Many small businesses are looking for space in this range. Each unit also has its own front door, AC unit, and bathroom.

An important factor is location. This building is on a main road in an expanding part of the county. My advertising to get new tenants has consisted of putting a large sign out by the road. See picture.

I decided on a color combination of red and yellow so it is noticeable when cars drive by. I have never had to do any advertising to get tenants, which is nice. Another question I ask myself when analyzing a property is would I rent space here for my business.

Two months after I purchased the property, Hurricane Charley ripped half the roof off and damaged all the signage, among other things. I remember driving to the property with my wife a day after the storm. On the way I started thinking my wife might be upset if she saw our building all torn apart. I explained to her that no matter what the property looked like she should remember we had insurance. As we approached the property, we saw tree limbs and debris everywhere. The soffits on both buildings were completely gone, along with the cupolas for both buildings. There was now a giant hole in the roof of each building where the cupolas used to be. It looked bad, and my wife became a little emotional at the first sight of the damage. I guess it is human nature.

Do not go one day without your property or business being insured. You never know what will happen. Commercial property insurance and business insurance are relatively inexpensive. There should be enough coverage to rebuild the property as well as, in my opinion, at least one million in liability coverage.

Make sure the company you purchase the insurance from has a high stability rating from Moody's or S&P. Moody's and S&P rate companies on their strength or likelihood they will go out of business. It will do no good to have insurance if the company goes out of business due to a bad storm or hurricane. Get at least three quotes to find your best deal.

Another incident that proved to be a learning experience was when a pipe broke in the wall at one of the offices. The office was flooded within minutes. All the flooring was ruined. Again, this building was insured, and we fixed the flooring in one week with as little disruption to the business as possible.

The second day after the leak I started hearing the word "mold" among the business owners. Don't get me wrong, mold can be a problem. In most cases, however, it is blown way out of proportion. This is another reason I wanted to dry up the floor and get the new flooring in as soon as possible.

At this time a business owner three doors down called to tell me there was mold in the bathroom. The leak was nowhere near this unit, but the owner had the word mold in her mind so all of a sudden she had a mold issue. She had been leasing the space for two years. Upon viewing the bathroom, I saw two quarter size black spots. I knew from experience there was not a mold problem, but the tenant was not going to just believe me.

I cut out all of the sheet rock (drywall) from the floor to two feet up. I asked the tenant to look inside the walls for any sign of mold. There was no mold. The walls were repaired. Even though this cost me money and I realized it was a waste of time, I also knew the tenant was not going to get mold off her mind until I proved to her there was no mold. The business owner went back to being a happy tenant telling everyone I was great. If I had not done anything about the mold, even though it was a waste of time, the tenant would have continued telling everyone she had mold problems that I was not correcting. The "so called" mold issue could have spread to other businesses. There would have been a negative vibe or attitude spreading through the office building. Sometimes you have to do things that make people happy for the long term good.

A couple of years ago I learned from a tenant that the following was living in the attic.

YES, A RACCOON.

It had fallen thru the drop ceiling into the:

YES, TOILET.

Fortunately there was good timing in this situation. The lady had just stood up and flushed the toilet. Had the lady decided to sit on the toilet 20 seconds longer she would have had a large pregnant raccoon in her lap. What a shocker that would have been. Fortunately the raccoon only fell into the toilet and the lady ran out of the bathroom screaming. The raccoon had fallen though the drop ceiling above. About 10 raccoons had gotten through the soffit and set up a home in the attic to have baby raccoons. We trapped all the raccoons and moved them 20 miles down the street. Those 20 seconds made the difference between having a good laugh and having a very upset tenant.

Lady Lake

This property in Lady Lake, FL was one of the first properties I looked at many years ago. At the time I was still the owner of Evans Insurance and had just started to learn about commercial properties.

I had a property developer friend go out to this property with me to give me some advice. The seller was asking $500,000 for this 7,000 square foot strip center. The property was run down but structurally sound, and it was in an above average area. All of the a/c systems looked old and in very poor condition. After reviewing everything about the property, I did not purchase it because of the a/c systems. Looking back, I believe that was a dumb reason for not purchasing the property.

One month after dismissing this property as unacceptable due to the a/c systems, I called the realtor back to say I would like to purchase the property for $500,000. The realtor told me the owner no longer wanted to sell. I started calling the realtor back every month to ask if the owner had changed his mind. About one year later the owner finally changed his mind, but he now wanted $600,000. The new price was still a good deal, so the contract was signed two days later before the owner changed his mind again.

Shortly after signing the contract, the owner did have second thoughts. He increased the asking price by $100,000 on the MLS listing, Loopnet, and the Property Source Book. Loopnet is the most popular online website to learn of commercial properties for sale. The owner was also not returning phone calls to me or the broker. He was now thinking he had under-priced the property, and he was right.

While I was inspecting the property with an in-spection company, a realtor was showing the prop-erty to another buyer. I asked the realtor what was going on and told her the property was already under contract. She was surprised and did not seem to be-lieve me. The owner had hired a new real estate bro-ker to sell this property. I informed the realtor again that this property was sold with the closing planned in about 20 days.

After meeting the new realtor, I called the original realtor who had helped me sign the contract to tell him the owner was obviously not cooperating, was ig-noring us, and was actively trying to sell the property for a higher price. The owner wanted us to go away. Unfortunately for him, we had a signed contract. What should I do next? The owner was not cooperating, and it is always difficult to purchase a property without both the buyer and the seller concurring.

Yes, I could contact an attorney and start paying $150-$200 per hour for legal assistance. My realtor knew the property owner's attorney, and we were guessing that he was going to use him for this transaction. I called the attorney and explained to him that we had a fully signed contract and were going to purchase the property but had not been able to contact the owner over the last week. I also explained that the owner was still actively marketing and showing the property, and we were afraid he was trying to back out of our deal. After this talk with the owner's attorney, the owner started communicating with us again. Apparently the attorney contacted the owner and explained to him that there was a legally binding contract for the sale of the property and that he could not just pretend a contract was not signed. Fifteen days later I purchased the property.

I updated the property with several new a/c systems and also put stucco on the front of the building along with a fresh coat of paint and new electric signs above each unit. The stucco, paint, and signs vastly improved the look of the building, and it was relatively inexpensive. The tenants were so happy they did not seem to mind a small increase in rent. The local city has a beautification committee that nominated me for *Improved Property of the Year*. I felt like I was the local hero for bringing this property back to life.

The property remained fully leased for the first two years with only one constant complaint coming from the tenants. The complaint was that the dirt and gravel parking lot in back of the building was unacceptable. I decided to do something about it. I received three quotes to pave this small ten space parking lot and picked a $10,000 quote from a company I felt would do a good job. The asphalt parking lot was completed. The lot looked good, and the tenants loved it.

Unfortunately, five weeks later I was notified that the city did not care for the new parking lot. The problem was I did not pull the proper permit. The city not only wanted a permit but also approval from the local water management council verifying that the retention pond was large enough so there would not be any flooding at the property. I asked if someone from the city could meet me at the property so they could see with their own eyes that the retention pond was four times as big as the parking lot and the property would not flood in a million years. The city refused to meet me and reiterated that I needed approval of the local water management district.

I contacted an engineer who dealt with these water issues to find out how to get this resolved. The engineer told me that since the water council was a government entity the approval process could easily take six months or more and cost me $20,000 in engineering and legal fees. I was also informed that if I applied for approval to the water management council they would evaluate the entire property not just the back area with the small parking lot. Their evaluation would be to see if the property met the government's flooding standards. What I learned was that after the evaluation took place, it was possible I would have to tear up all of the front parking lot if I did not meet government flooding standards.

The ruling by the water management council had the potential of literally destroying the property and forcing the tenants to move out. The power of government. Amazing! I saw this issue as conceivably turning into a large problem for me. I contacted the asphalt company that installed the parking lot and had them remove it the following week. The issue with the city was resolved, and the tenants were back to the dirt and gravel parking lot. I was back to a happy Government with unhappy Tenants.

I was so fed up after this issue that I decided to sell. Looking back, I realize this was probably an overreaction. I found a buyer at a price of $875,000, and this property was sold. The lesson I took from this experience was that when you are looking at a property to purchase and the parking lot is gravel, keep in mind that it may not be easy or possible to install a parking lot due to government regulations and the permits that are required.

Negotiating

The art of negotiating a deal is an art. Like anything else, the more you negotiate the better you become at the process. Be willing to walk away from a deal at any time if the deal is not right or, even if it is right, turns bad at the end and you are about to close and purchase the property. Do not fall in love with property; remember you are purchasing it to make money. Stay calm while you are negotiating. The other side will not be able to tell what you are thinking. Slow down the process. The other side may become concerned that you are losing interest in the deal. You want the buyer or seller to be more motivated than you. Buying a property at the right price is obviously very important. Having said the above statements, let me add that you want to also remain flexible.

For example, let's say your maximum bid for a property is $495,000 and the seller refuses to go below $500,000, do the deal. It is close enough.

Here's another example: Let's say there is a property listed for $400,000 and you want to pay

$360,000. You offer $340,000 and the seller counters at $350,000. This is good, correct? Just say YES. Maybe not. It may be wise to counter at $348,500 and say this is the highest I can go. If you had accepted $350,000, the seller might start thinking he countered too low and have second thoughts. If he rejects your $348,500 offer, you can still accept the $350,000 offer. Now he knows you would not go any higher. Of course, if there are several bids coming in on a property, do not play these games.

A different scenario would be if the property is a great deal at $400,000. Not only accept the deal at that price, go find the real estate broker and immediately sign the contract before someone changes his mind.

Each deal is different, and as you become better at negotiating you will become aware of these nuances during the process.

Winter Haven

This commercial property came up for sale one morning as I was looking through my list of new properties on the market. I knew this property was a good deal because it was a 12,000 square foot retail center, fully leased, and very close to the Cypress Gardens Amusement Park. Within an hour I was in my car to make the 90 minute trip to the property. This property was selling for $83 per square foot for a total of $1,000,000, a good price in 2005. The property needed a little updating. Most importantly however, it was structurally sound and located in an above average location. This was a bargain. From the parking lot I dialed the real estate agent to tell him I would like to make an offer.

The broker informed me, "It's already sold."

"How can it be sold already? It was just listed five hours ago." I said.

The broker and I ended up talking for about an hour on the phone while I was sitting in the car at the property. I ended the conversation by telling the broker I would like to do a full price back up offer. He said he would fax over the backup contract. One week went by. I did not receive the backup offer contract, so I called the agent back and asked if he was still going to send it to me.

He then told me about the games the buyer was playing. The buyer did not want to pay the state fees, amounting to about $9,000, associated with the transaction. Normally the seller pays this state fee, but everything is negotiable. The buyer had faxed the contract back to the broker without signing it. It was at this point that I had happened to call the broker back.

The broker asked me, "Do you want the deal? I am tired of playing games with the other buyer."

My response was, "Of course."

By the end of the day I had a contract on the property. It was a full price offer of $1,000,000, and I was going to be paying the $9,000 dollar state fee. It was such a good deal I was not concerned with the $9,000 dollar state fee, and I had not even looked at the leases. The contract gave me 20 days due diligence to look over the property, so I could get out of it for any reason during the first 20 days. For right now the important thing was the contract was signed.

We closed 30 days later. The inspection went well with just some minor issues, and I met the lender, with whom I had developed a relationship, at the property and was able to get financing. Since you never know for sure about the financing, I met with two local bankers near the property regarding the financing. I brought them a 50 page packet which explained everything about the property and also included such things as my resume and tax returns. I discussed the benefits of financing the property with each lender and even dressed in a full suit to impress them. I was declined in both instances, but the community banker I had a relationship with came through and financed the deal.

After closing is when the work started. I renovated the property with some stucco work, painted, resealed and restriped the parking lot, and did some landscape work. The hard part was getting the tenants to sign a new lease since most of the current leases were out of date and most of the tenants had gotten into the habit of paying their rent whenever they wanted to.

One tenant in particular gave me a rough time with delay after delay, excuse after excuse on why he could not sign a new lease. This went on for a couple of months until finally I gave him three more days and verbally called him and said, "This is the final deadline. If you do not sign a new lease, we will start the eviction process."

Two days later he returned my lease back to me via his attorney. The attorney had basically re-written every paragraph I had in the lease and added an additional 10 pages.

I told the tenant, "This is unacceptable at this point. I am not going to go back and forth with attorneys so I can get a large attorney bill. My lease is my lease. If you want to make one or two basic changes, that I can understand. I could probably agree to that but, if not, you will need to sign my lease or the eviction process will start tomorrow."

Within an hour I had my signed lease.

This property ended up being a great property. I owned it for two years, never lost a tenant and was able to sell it for almost 1.5 million. A roughly $400,000 profit in two years. Not bad, huh?

While I was trying to sell the property, I was still having second thoughts about selling since I normally like to buy and hold and keep receiving the monthly income. My thoughts for selling were to take some money off the table for something else because I was too heavily invested in just real estate. At the inspection, the buyer brought in a handyman, electrician, plumber, roofer, etc. Ten minutes after the inspection started, the ac guy started walking back to where the buyer's agent and I were standing.

I said to myself, "here we go."

Sure enough the contractor's response was that we needed two new ac systems in back.

The buyer's agent turned to me and said, "So, you will install two new systems?"

I said, "No, I am not installing any new systems. As a matter of fact, I am not going to make any repairs. It will be **as is**. If you do not want the property, we can just call the deal off because I do not really even want to sell."

After this I did not hear anything else regarding me paying for any repairs with the property. I could tell from the buyer's actions he really wanted this property. I felt it was worth the risk to tell him I would not be spending money on repairs. In this case I had the upper hand since the buyer wanted to purchase more than I wanted to sell.

Timing is everything

Yes, I had good timing in making the follow-up call to the broker that ultimately landed me the deal. But this deal would not have happened if my phone communication skills were not good. In my first phone call I was able to develop a good rapport and trust with the broker that I was a good person with whom to do a property transaction. Yes, good timing can be lucky, but you must put yourself in a position to take advantage of the luck. I define luck as **opportunity met with preparation.** During that second phone call, when the broker asked me if I wanted the deal, I had enough knowledge of the commercial property industry to say yes instantly. All those hours of researching properties and miles driven to different properties had just paid off.

Around the same time as the last property purchase, I entered into a contract to purchase a small office plaza in Punta Gorda, Florida. On paper this property fit the criteria I had in mind. In this particular case, I sent a purchase contract over first without looking at the property since it was a six hour drive (round trip) to view the property. If the owner rejected my offer, I would just move on to the next property and not waste a day driving to look at this one. The owner accepted my offer in this instance, and we entered into a binding contract. Of course, I had 20 days due diligence to get out of the deal. The seller, on the other hand, could not legally get out of the deal. I decided to go look at the property the next Monday.

During the weekend, however, I found another property that would work better for me and decided to get out of the Punta Gorda deal with the due diligence clause. For whatever reason, I decided to wait until Wednesday of the next week to call the broker to tell him the property was not suitable for me. As luck would have it, I received a call from the owner on Tuesday saying he had made a mistake and did not want to sell the property after all. You guessed right! I now wanted to purchase the property, and we still had a legal contract allowing me to do so. If he had just waited one more day, I would have cancelled the contract and it would have been terminated. The seller ended up paying me $15,000 to get out of the deal. Not bad for doing nothing. Timing was good in this situation.

Small storage facility

I located a small storage facility in the Tampa Bay, Florida area. The cash flow seemed good, and it was in a growing area. The purchase price was $500,000 with a deposit of $12,000. On the last day of due diligence, the day I could cancel the contract and get my deposit money back, a lender verbally assured me they could do the deal. I was told they could not send a written confirmation because the vice president of commercial lending had to sign off on the deal, and he was out of town. They reassured me over and over again that this deal was no problem; they could definitely do it. So I did not cancel the contract, and my due diligence was over.

Three days later the loan officer called. "I made a mistake," he stated, "I cannot do the deal."

I soon found out that finding a loan for this small storage facility would be difficult. One loan officer told me his concern was that a large company would come into the area and build a huge facility. They would then set the prices so low it could drive the small operators of storage facilities out of business.

This made sense to me since the location of a storage facility is not as important as the location of a retail strip center. Based on this, I decided to lose my security deposit and move on to another deal.

What I learned was that sometimes you will lose money by taking a risk; this is going to happen. I also learned to commit to lower deposits unless I am trying to prove to an owner I am serious about purchasing a property. Sometimes presenting an offer with a large deposit check attached to it can make a difference. I also learned to get a written commitment letter from a lender stating they will do the loan. A verbal commitment does not guarantee anything.

When purchased, it looked like this:

After updating:

Sometimes the best way to purchase a property is to just contact the property owner directly. I contacted the owner of the Bunker Hill strip center and asked if he wanted to sell. The owner was older and said he would sell for $2,000,000, which was way above the $1,400,000 I thought it was worth. This started a conversation that went back and forth for six months. After a year we still could not agree on price, but it was becoming evident that the older gentleman was going to need help in managing the property.

The owner's son asked if I could help with the bookkeeping. I agreed to start managing the property for him, not for the little amount of money I received each month, but so eventually I could purchase the property. Six months into managing the property, I was accused by a local real estate agent of illegally managing a commercial property because I did not have a real estate license. The owner of the property and I contacted an attorney to look into this claim. The attorney came back with an inconclusive answer; he said it was a gray area in the law. I decided to tell the property owner I could not manage his property because I was not sure if I was doing something illegal and did not want to risk it.

It only took a few days for the property owner to call me back and let me know he was ready to sell for the price I had offered. The contract was signed, and we closed four weeks later. I updated the property with new paint, stucco work, new signage, and a new 500 gallon water tank for the well.

After picking the new paint color, one tenant complained profusely that I had lost my mind if I was going to paint the building that color. I re-evaluated but still decided that the paint color I had chosen would be best for the building.

If there is one thing that seems to be difficult and takes a lot of time to figure out, it is picking the right paint colors. Remember, you will not make everyone happy with the paint color you have chosen. A good way to find paint colors that are in style is to ask a painter. He or she is painting every day and should know the latest trends in paint colors. Another way to pick out paint colors is to hire an exterior designer. The local paint shops will be able to recommend and refer you to the right people to help pick out paint colors. Hiring an exterior designer will cost you money. Over the years I have found I can pick out paint colors as well as an exterior designer. The time consuming way to pick out paint colors is to go to Home Depot, pick up 100 sample colors and whittle it down from there. One last comment, a paint color on a little swatch will look better or worse when it is on the building.

The tenants took a few weeks to adapt to the way I managed the property. I required a new lease if the current one was terminated and made it clear that the lease payments were due on the first day of the month and would be considered late if the payment was not received by the 10th day of the month. The tenants eventually became used to paying during the first week of the month and not when they felt like it. You want your tenant to feel that his lease payment is the most important bill to pay and that it should be paid before the water, electric, and any other bill.

The property next to ours was a convenience store. Due to the way the properties sit, many people used our parking lot as a cut through to get to the convenience store. This caused two problems for our property. The constant flow of cars was a liability issue for people walking in the parking lot, and there were constantly teenagers wandering onto our property while hanging out around the convenience store.

One wood fence ended this problem. See pictures below.

On the day the fence was being installed, one of the business owners (tenants) came out. In a loud voice he told me that I was out of my mind to put a fence up that blocked traffic and that it would become too difficult for customers to get to our property. He said that he may have to move or go out of business.

Calmly I explained, "It's just a fence. Let's give it a try, and if it causes problems we will take it down in a couple of weeks."

Less than one week later the same business owner called to tell me that the fence was a great idea after all. There was no longer a constant flow of cars, and no teenagers were hanging out on the property. It probably helped business because customers did not have to be concerned about tattooed teenagers or other problems that might be encountered.

M y first billboard.

After I purchased the property, the first thing I did was sign a contract with Clear Channel. They agreed to build the billboard and would also pay me $500 per month to lease the ground underneath the billboard. The monthly payment is now up to $700 per month and growing since the area is in an economic growth area. This is a nice asset because I literally have to do nothing and will get a check every month from Clear Channel. A lot of cities and counties have been changing their laws and not allowing new Billboards. After the purchase of a property, I always check with the county to see if billboards are allowed.

In 2007, I spotted a 4,000 square foot strip center for sale. See pic below. This property I was well aware of because I used to drive by it every day on my way to work. I liked the way it looked with the large porch out front. It looked inviting. I was familiar with the property when it went up for sale.

I called the owner, who was also the listing agent; the property was listed for $700,000. After looking over the property, including the financials, I offered $500,000. The offer was declined without a counter offer. Six months went by. I called the owner back and found out he would sell for $650,000 now. I told them that price would still not work for me. I called back six months later. He would now sell for $600,000. Still not good enough. Another year went by, and I followed up with a phone call. I learned he would now sell for $500,000. Good news! Right? No, not good news.

By this time the real estate market had collapsed. I did another analysis of the property and determined the current value was $350,000; of course, the owner rejected my offer. He should have accepted my offer of $500,000 two years earlier.

Another year went by so it was now the summer of 2010, and I decided to give the owner another phone call. The phone number I had been using was now disconnected so I decided to take a drive to the property and check it out. While talking with a few of the tenants I learned that the owner had retired and moved to Kentucky. I was also told that the bank was foreclosing on the property.

The tenants were unhappy because the general maintenance at the property was becoming neglected. They were especially discontented that the septic system was in poor condition and needed to be replaced. This current news was good for me, the potential buyer. One of the tenants gave me the owner's new phone number in Kentucky. I called the owner and was told he would now sell the property for $425,000. He was in agreement that the septic had to be replaced at a cost of $25,000. I offered $325,000, with the owner replacing the septic system.

The negotiations went back and forth over the next two months without an agreement. I was in the driver's seat since I knew the owner was getting close to foreclosure. The owner's final offer was $275,000, but he wanted me to hand him an additional $50,000 in cash in the parking lot after closing. I think this is illegal, definitely unethical. He wanted the cash outside of closing because whatever amount was collected at closing was going to the bank to pay down the lien, and he would receive nothing.

The first question one would ask is, "how was the owner going bankrupt if this strip center is fully leased?" He had taken out one large loan with several properties involved. Even though this particular property was doing well, the owner's properties as a whole were not.

The lesson learned here was to keep property loans completely separated. A bank will attempt to add in other properties as collateral. I would not do it unless you have no other choice and are looking to purchase a great deal.

As the deal continued to progress toward bankruptcy, I contacted the lender to let them know I was interested in purchasing the property when it was foreclosed. I heard nothing for two more months, and then one day in December 2010 I received a call from a real estate broker who was representing the bank. This call pertained to this Mt. Dora property.

He said, "I heard through the grapevine you want to purchase the strip center."

I replied, "You heard correct."

His next question was, "What price do you want to pay?"

The thought that quickly ran through my head was that I wanted to pay as low a price as possible but not get ridiculous with the offer and lose the deal.

I was thinking about an offer of $275,000 but blurted out, "How about $250,000?"

The broker said that was about the price he was thinking. We ended up agreeing to a price of $255,000, and the bank also replaced the septic system and paid $10,000 to replace some rotten wood and replace a broken a/c system.

Ten days after signing the contract I received the results of the survey I ordered. See next page.

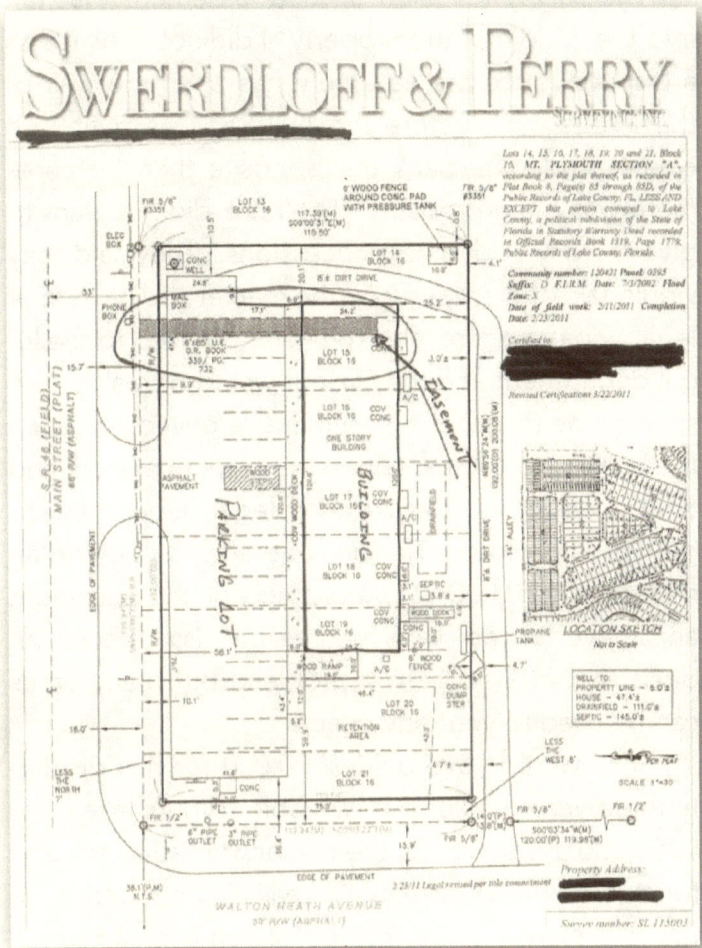

The survey revealed a utility easement that ran into the middle of the property. I did not think it was a big deal since the easement has been there since the 1960's, well before the building was built. Of course I told the bank the opposite that the easement was a big problem. The bank did not want to give me any additional concessions. They said they would take the property off the market and have their legal department resolve the issue. I talked to the legal department and they said it would probably take six months to get the easement removed. I called the bank back and explained the amount of work and time it was going to take their legal department to get issue resolved. The bank agreed to give me an additional $10,000 if I would accept the easement and move forward with the closing. Issues arise on deals that at first seem a problem, but many times can be used to your advantage.

So, I would have paid $500,000 for this property three years earlier but was able to purchase it for $255,000. Back in 2007 the owner wanted to sell and retire. He should have been realistic and sold it for the real market value instead of some dream price that never happened. If you really want or need to sell your property, be realistic on the price. If it has not sold in six weeks, you are asking too much or maybe you need to do some maintenance.

Six months after purchasing the property I decided to take out a loan on the property. Why would I do this if the property was purchased with cash? I did a new loan for $200,000 to free up equity to purchase a new property when a good deal comes along. I now own a property with only $55,000 of my own money put into the deal.

Let's take a financial look at this deal.

Purchase price	$ 255,000.00
new loan	$ 200,000.00
amount invested	$ 55,000.00

Gross income (yearly)	$ 48,000.00

Expenses

Loan pmt	$ 18,000.00
property taxes	$ 4,000.00
property insurance	$ 1,700.00
electric	$ 1,600.00
water treatment	$ 1,560.00
garbage pickup	$ 1,764.00
landscaping	$ 2,100.00
Total	$ 30,724.00

Net Income	$ 17,276.00

Return on Investment (17276/55000)= 31% return on money

Also, the debt on the loan is being paid down. I am gaining a good tax deduction because the IRS allows me to depreciate the property.

Recently I was working on purchasing a 17,000 square foot retail property. Here is a picture of the property and the flyer I mailed out to surrounding businesses after it was purchased.

It is a property that was built in 1990. The property was for sale five years ago for $1.2 million. One year ago it was listed for sale again at $825,000 on a short sale. It is a short sale because the owner owes more than the property is worth. I contacted the real estate agent to gather information on the property. After my evaluation I told the realtor the property was worth about $560,000, in my opinion. The realtor said the owner would not go lower than $825,000 on the price. I thanked the realtor for her time and told her when the price gets to the $500,000 range to give me a call back.

One year later I received a call saying they had just reduced the price to $550,000. I verified that all of the same tenants were still leasing at the property even though it was only 50% leased out. We wrote up the contract for $550,000. The owner owed about $1,000,000 on the property. Then we waited; we could not move forward with due diligence until the bank accepted our offer which was a lot less than the note on the property. The process of the bank accepting our offer or even responding can take several months. It only took two weeks in this case, and the bank surprisingly accepted our offer without even making a counter offer.

The inspection was particularly interesting because some of the units in the building we went into had been locked up for several years. What we saw in these units was a blanketed carpet of these:

PALMETTO BUGS.

A lot of people just call them a cockroach. Fortunately, they were all dead. The water in the toilets had dried up many years prior, and my best guess was that the palmetto bugs were able to get into the units through the toilets and then could not find a way out and died. It was literally a carpet of bugs. The bugs were disgusting but would have no factor in the decision to purchase because they were just bugs and could be swept away. The inspection found no structural problems, which is always my main concern.

Our 30 day due diligence began. The inspection, survey, and appraisal went well. It was about five days before the due diligence was over. This was where I played some poker and tried to get a better deal. I started getting a vibe from the realtor that the lender really wanted to unload this property and was willing to negotiate further. So why not try to get a better deal? I had nothing to lose. If the bank denied my request, I was still going forward with the deal. The bank did not know that though. I had to be careful with the words I used because I did not want to say "if my demands are not met I am cancelling the con-tract". However, I wanted to be firm enough with the lender so they knew I was serious with my request and may walk away from the deal (even though I was definitely purchasing). Here is the exact email I sent to the realtor:

"Hi Sue, after inspecting the property, including the roof, it is going to take 40k for me to bring the property up to an acceptable level. Please notify the lender of my request of 40k to be paid to me at closing. If you can find out from the lender if this is acceptable by Thursday (3 days from now) that would be great since I have 2 other properties in the Orlando area that I am interested in pursuing if the bank cannot agree to the 40k. If this is acceptable to the bank I can close in 2 weeks from today."

To my shock, two days later the bank agreed to pay my $40,000 at closing. Little did they know that I was bluffing about cancelling the contract and was still going to purchase the property with or without the $40,000. I would say this was a pretty good hand of poker.

During this same time, the bank I was getting a loan from had guaranteed a loan with the terms of 30% down and 15 year amortization. I wanted a loan with 25% down and 20 year amortization to keep my monthly payments as low as possible. After the appraisal came in $100,000 higher than the sales price of the property, the lender allowed me to put 25% down but still insisted on the 15 year amortization. What could I do now? It seemed as though I was going to have to accept the 15 year amortization.

After some further thought, I offered to put $30,000 in a checking account at the bank if they would agree to the 20 year amortization. The $30,000 could only be used for improvements to the property. I was planning on spending $30,000 on the property during the first month anyway. By thinking outside the box I was able to think of a way to talk the bank into agreeing to the 20 year amortization.

Fast Forward 2 years

Two years later I had updated the property inside and out. The landscaping was looking good, and I had also managed to lease out two additional spaces. However, there still remained three vacant spaces. I could not get any more spaces leased out no matter what I did. The same complaint I was hearing every time I showed the space was that the space was too large. Two thousand square feet spaces were difficult to lease out in this particular market. I also realized this property was located in a dead zone. I like to call a dead zone an area that is depressed with no immediate or long term outlook for economic growth and activity. I thought this property was a good deal since I was paying such a low price per square foot. I was wrong, and that is why property location is one of the first things I consider when looking at a potential property to purchase.

I listed the property for $795,000 in January, 2013 even though my real estate broker recommended $695,000. After six months I lowered the price to $745,000 and then to $695,000 six months later.

Investors were looking at the property but, with no offers, the asking price was too high. I should have listened to the advice of my agent. After lowering the price to $695,000, I started receiving offers in the $550,000 range. This was the purchase price for the property, and once I deducted broker fees I would be losing money on the deal. I finally received an offer of $600,000. I decided to accept it and move on. After verbally agreeing to the price, another 2 weeks went by without receiving the signed copy of the contract. At this point I managed to find a new tenant. A new tenant increases the income of the property; thus, it should increase the sales price. I told my broker that since I have a new tenant I should get at least $625,000 for the property. The buyer would not increase his offer, and I was beginning to wonder if he would ever purchase. Due to the in-creased income, I received a cash offer of $675,000 from an international buyer. The buyer waived the inspection and closed quickly. **You have to like that**.

Six months after closing, the buyer (new owner) called me with a question about the property. During the conversation I asked how things were going.

He said, "We have lost two tenants, and that is a hard location to find new tenants."

I thought to myself, no kidding and that is why I sold the property.

Handyman

As owner of the property, you need to verify that work has been done and done correctly. After small jobs are completed, I drive to the property to verify work has been done correctly. If a larger office renovation is taking place, I will usually hang out at the property to keep the workers on track. If I am not present, workers tend to get sidetracked, become lazy, forget what needs to be done, and many times just do things wrong. At the jobsite, I will write on a poster board the tasks that need to be done. I tape the poster board to the wall so they see it every time they walk by. If you cannot hang out at a property all day, stop by as many times as possible. Call the worker or contractor often to see how things are going and mention any issues right away so they can be addressed.

When my handyman is doing regular mainte-nance at a property, I usually stop by in the afternoon to see what he has accomplished. We then take a tour of the property to go over other work that needs to be done.

Once work is done, it is important to pay contractors as quickly as possible. Do not underestimate paying workers quickly. They will appreciate doing work for you and will be happy to accept the next job over other job offers. **Paying handymen and contractors quickly is very important.** Just today my handyman said he turned down work because it was too much of a hassle to get paid after work was done.

He then said to me, "Your checks are always good."

Here is a picture of Mike (my handyman) about to mow some grass. Unfortunately, two hours after this picture was taken, the riding mower caught on fire and burned to the ground. No injuries.

If it's too confusing, don't do it or (not)

In January, 2015, I finally found an office property to purchase. Here is the listing flyer:

CENTRAL FLORIDA PLAZA
4,560 SF Retail/Office Plaza For Sale

FL 33897

- Professional Plaza with Six (6) Demised Units with a Total of 4,560 SF.
- Private Offices with Restrooms in Each Unit
- Well-maintained Plaza Located on U.S. Hwy. 27 just South of U.S. Hwy. 192
- Conveniently Located South of the Polk/Lake County Line with Multiple Access Points to I-4 via U.S. Hwy. 27 or U.S. Hwy. 192
- Entire Property 4,560 SF offered at $675,000

Please Do Not Disturb Tenants - Call For An Appointment

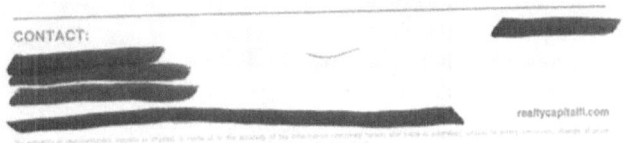

CONTACT:

realtycapitalfl.com

FLOOR PLAN AND LOCATOR MAP

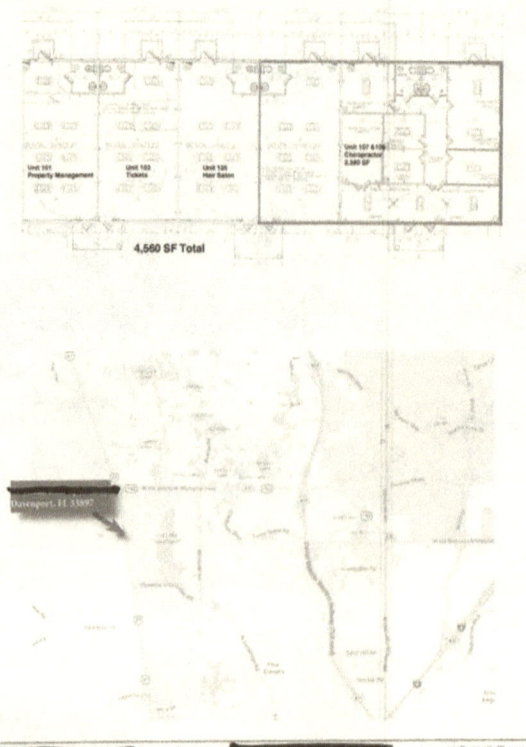

After my last property, I was determined that the correct location was of the upmost importance. This was an office property with six spaces with each space being 760 square feet for a total of 4560 square feet for the building. The property was on a major road close to Disney World. The road was currently being expanded to three lanes each way. A road expansion is probably the most obvious indication that the area is on the upswing and expecting a lot of future development. The area was alive, not dead like the last property I sold. Office spaces of 760 square feet are also nice size spaces to lease to small businesses. It is a manageable size to lease for the tenant and to maintain for the owner. The larger 2000 square foot spaces at the last property were too expensive for most small businesses to operate, and many walked away because of the size of the space. The sale price was $600,000, each space was $100.000.00. Each unit could be rented for $1000 to $1200 each per month. The numbers looked good, and the property inspection showed no problems with the property. Here is a better look at the property:

The lender was willing to lend money, but we then ran into a problem. The owner had set this property up as a condo association. So what, you might say, many properties have condo associations.

This property "kind of" has an association. So what does that mean? There were 10 units or office condos in the association with each having a separate parcel ID or identification number. We were purchasing one building with six units, and the other building had four units owned by someone else. Each office could be sold separately.

Now this is the confusing part. The association was not actually operating or functioning. The original owner was collecting dues from other condo owners and paying some bills. Where was the rest of the money going? You are probably getting confused about this deal because that is how I felt. The owner suggested I hire an attorney if I wanted to feel more comfortable with the deal. I suggested that it was now the owner's responsibility to make me feel comfortable with the deal.

One of my rules is that if I do not understand the deal, I am done with the deal. I am not going to call an attorney to try and explain it to me. The truth is the attorney would not know more about this than I do. At this point I gave the owner three days to clarify things. The three days passed with the owner not willing to clarify things. Was the owner hiding something? Who knows, but it was just not worth moving forward with this property with the deal this confusing. **Know when to walk away.**

After looking aggressively for three weeks and not finding a good property, my mind drifted back to the building with the condo association. I thought everything was good about the property. It had good size units, good location, and the building was not too old. I decided to take another look. I contacted the owner of the other building even though the seller didn't want me to. I ended up meeting with the owner of the other building, and I could tell she would be easy to work with. She wanted the association to run efficiently and not waste money. She would be agreeable with me running the association and did not want or require us to have a formal condo association meeting. I would technically have control since I would own six of the ten units.

One of the first things I would change after closing would be to find a new company to take care of the dumpster (garbage). The current owner was paying $400 per month to pick up a six-yard garbage container once per week. The company I had been using for other properties quoted me $98 per month for the same size dumpster.

Also, the association was paying a lot for city water. I heard many times that city water was expensive in this county, and that was just the way it was. It seemed to me the water bill was too high. There had to be a reason. I called the county and explained my thoughts about the water bill being too high. They listened as I said I felt there had to be a problem or some way to lower the bill. I found out the property was on a 1 ½-inch water meter, and the city charged a base rate based on the size of the meter before any water was used. Bottom line, I would be able to lower the water bill significantly simply by changing to a 1-inch meter.

At most properties there are things that can be done to reduce costs. Many property owners become lazy over time and do not keep costs down. I was happy that I would be able to get costs down and under control at this property.

I was not happy after I spoke with the attorney. Normally, I do not speak with attorneys unless it is absolutely necessary. However, my real estate broker kept insisting, so I agreed to it. The attorney told me, as usual, about all the rules, regulations, restrictions, and problems with condo associations. After speaking with the attorney for one hour, any normal person would have to be crazy to go forward with this deal. So I went forward with the deal. **LOL!**

The fact is that this is a small condo association, ten units with two owners who can work together to make it run smoothly. One of the things the attorney said was that we could not close for at least 30 days because the condo by-laws stated that for any board election there has to be a 30 day notice given to all owners. She said we would be breaking the law to close before we had an official board meeting. Yes, this is important with larger associations, but we had two owners who did not care about this rule. So after several months and lots of confusion over the condo association, I went forward and purchased the building. I paid $615,000, put down 20%, and received a loan for $492,000 at 4 ¼ percent for 10 years. The loan would be due in 10 years or we would need to refinance.

Here is a look at the financials:

Property analysis					
Purchase price		$ 615,000.00			
New Loan		$ 492,000.00			
Amt invested		$ 123,000.00			
Gross income (yearly)		$ 84,000.00			
Expenses:					
Loan pmt		$ 30,036.00			
Property taxes		$ 6,000.00			
Condo assoc dues		$ 12,000.00			
Total expenses:		$ 48,036.00			
Net income		$ 35,934.00			
Return on investmer		*29% return $35964/$123000*			

In 2013, I spotted a car wash facility for sale on an online auction site.

After driving by the property and the surrounding area, I thought it seemed to be an acceptable location. I also reviewed the marketing package and financials that were made available. The day of the online auction arrived, and I was determined that I would bid up to $100,000.00 for the car wash. In the final hour the bid went from $40,000 to a final sale price of $240,000.00, which was way past my final bid of $100,000.00. I thought this deal was over.

Two weeks later I received a call from the auction company saying the high bidder had decided not to purchase the car wash and wanting to know if I was still interested. I said yes and offered $75,000.00 cash. I received a counter offer of $150,000.00. We finally agreed on a price of $125,000.00, and I had to make a $20,000.00 deposit within 48 hours. **This is where I made my mistake.** Did I forget to say that this $20,000.00 deposit was non-refundable? I decided to make this deposit solely based on driving by the car wash and looking at some basic financials. The due diligence period, the important part of the deal, I was willing to forgo. **What was I thinking?** And, in the end I would lose the $20,000.00.

What could I have done differently? I could have refused to make the deposit non- refundable until I had 30 days to do my due diligence. Yes, I could have lost the deal. I could have also said I would only make a $5,000.00 non-refundable deposit. I thought this car wash was such a good deal I did not put enough thought into this non-refundable deposit. Bottom line, I made a mistake. It is going to happen. **But I will not make this mistake again**.

A few days after making the deposit, I was able to meet the real estate broker at the property to inspect the property. The first problem with the property was that vandals had gotten into the main building and cut all of the electric wires to steal copper.

A day later I contacted the county to verify that there would not be a problem to turn on city water to the property.

The response was, "Yes, there is a problem that needs to be resolved before the city will turn on the water."

The problem was there was no retention pond at the property. I then found out that the prior owner of the car wash had sold the property next to this piece of property one year ago. The retention pond was on the property that was sold, and now the county wanted a new retention pond somewhere on the property before they would turn on the water. While talking to an engineer, I learned that one of the car wash bays would have to be removed so the new retention pond could be installed. This new retention pond would cost about $75,000.

The most obvious question at this point would be: Why didn't you call the county about the water before now? The answer would be: I did.

Two weeks earlier I had called the county and asked the same question about starting water service.

At that time I was told, "No problem. Just let us know which day to start water service."

The question was repeated just so I could be certain, "Are you absolutely sure turning on the water will not be a problem?"

"I am positive," was the response that came back.

Two weeks later, once my $20,000 was not refundable, I heard a different answer.

A few days later a real estate broker friend agreed to spend the day driving to the property and evaluating the surrounding area to determine if this car wash was a good investment. The first place we stopped at was another car wash three miles from the property we were looking at. This car wash was a new, modern one with the express tunnel type of car wash. The sign outside said "3 minute wash for $3 dollars, plus you stay in your car".

We got out of our car to see if the attendant would talk with us. He was more than happy to tell us everything we wanted to know about the car wash business. He told us his car wash was doing 300-400 cars per day. We told him we were looking to purchase the car wash down the street, fix it up and get it running again. He was not concerned with the competition. He said the type and style of the car wash we were purchasing was outdated and delivered an inferior wash to his new express tunnel, plus customers like to stay in their cars and not sit in a waiting room.

After finding out all of the issues with this car wash, I decided my best decision was to forfeit the $20,000 and walk away from the deal. Losing $20,000 was painful but was the best decision. If I had not admitted to myself that I made a mistake, I would have went on to make a larger mistake and lose a lot more than $20,000.

One month later I was called by the broker saying I could now buy the property for $45,000. I still had to decline. This car wash was a loser. It would have been a money pit.

Recently I have become interested in shipping containers.

The shipping containers have become another monthly source of income. Of course you need some land to put them on. The containers are made of steel so there is very little maintenance, and I am finding that many businesses are in need of storage space. The containers cost $3500 each, and I am getting $900 every six months ($150 per month) for rent. My $3500 investment generates $1800 per year or a 51% return. I will get my money back in two years. After the two years, it is pure profit.

I make each tenant sign a one-year lease agreement which states the lease amount, of course, but also states that the tenant is responsible for all vandalism and theft to the tenant's personal property while stored in the shipping container. The tenant is also responsible for all liability of any nature inside the container.

I like to purchase the new shipping containers even though they are a little more expensive. They look good and are not all rusted out and dented. The new containers keep my property looking good. This is another asset that produces a monthly income.

New Opportunity

During one of my property purchases I was referred to a local title insurance agency for the closing. They did such a good job that I started using them on every property transaction that I could; of course, the seller normally decides which title company will close the transaction. But, remember, everything is negotiable. As the years went by I began to get to know the closers of this particular title insurance office. It became obvious to me that they were well known in the community, did many transactions each month, and made a lot of money for the large company for which they worked.

I approached the managers (closers) that I knew and asked if they would like to start a new title insurance business. My offer was that I would invest $100,000.00 to help get the business up and running. They would be leaving a large national company to start a small title office from scratch. I kept asking on and off over a two year time frame.

In August 2009 I purchased an office condo and thought that this would be a good place to open a title insurance office. I had not talked with the two managers for about six months, but this would be a good time to make one more call. This call would prove to be good timing. Employees of the local office where the managers worked were being forced to work through a national call center. To call someone at that local office first you had to speak with someone at the national call center and then they would, hopefully, forward you to the right person at the right office in a timely manner. Is this bad customer service or what? You would think a large national company would not goof up like this.

With the company going to the call center, the two managers took my offer, and we began making plans to start a new title insurance agency. Our plan was to be open for business in December 2009. In the middle of November the large title company found out about our plans through the grapevine and fired the entire staff instantly. We had not done anything illegal, and the employees were all going to give their two week notice.

Approximately three weeks before we were going to open, all of the employees were standing there at the new office, looking at me as I walked in. At this point we had no computers, telephone system or copiers. One bright spot, we did have furniture. Within ten days we were up and running. It has now been six years since we opened the title insurance business. Things are going well.

There are a lot of opportunities out there. Sometimes just by keeping your eyes and ears open you will find a good opportunity.

Here is a picture of the Title Insurance office

Self-storage deal

In 2014, I found a self-storage facility on Loopnet that was for sale in an above average area. Years ago I had told myself that I was done with self-storage facilities after I lost my $10,000 security deposit on a different property. I drove by the property and looked at some financials that were pretty vague. The owners would not meet with me or give me any additional info unless we agreed on a price. The real estate agent suggested that I should just make an offer, pending 30-day due diligence, just to get the ball rolling. The asking price was $875,000. Based upon the info I had, I offered $575,000. Surprisingly, the seller came all the way down to $675,000 with his counteroffer.

Shortly after signing the contract for $675,000, we met the real estate agent and seller at the property. The property looked like an office building from the outside since all of the storage units were on the inside. The outside landscaping was in poor condition with all the landscaping about dead due to lack of water. As we walked in, we were surprised to find the inside of the building looked brand new. Usually the outside of the property gives you a good idea on how the inside looks; this property was the exception. The seller had a full time person who worked the front desk.

My first question was, "What does your employee do all day?"

I asked this because on average they only leased one or two units per week in addition to the customers who stopped by to make payments.

The seller's response to my question was, "Good question. I do not know what our employee does all day."

As we walked through the building, we observed that everything was new and in good working order. One other item of curiosity that we noticed was that the seller did not believe in computers. Everything in the business was handwritten and, even though it was organized, it seemed crazy that they had not entered the 21st century and started operating the business more efficiently.

The seller was also reluctant to provide us with the full financials since he seemed to be a very private person. After another week I finally received the full financials and copies of all the leases. One thing I noticed was he was not collecting sales tax. In Florida, sales tax for rental property needs to be collected and paid to the government monthly. The sales tax rate in Florida is six to seven percent. So, even though he was not collecting sales tax, it still had to be paid monthly to the government. This basically made their financials seven percent weaker due to the sales tax issue.

I know there are owners of real estate who do not file and pay the monthly sales tax to the government that is required. **I would not operate like that.** Keep it legal, collect the sales tax, and mail it to the government as required by law.

The decision to move forward and purchase the property came down to one question: Could we operate the self-storage facility without an employee? Having to pay an employee made the expenses too high and the net income too low. Of course with no employees, the net income looked pretty good. Through more research and talking to a property manager who specialized in self-storage facilities, I found my answer. For hiring an employee to make sense, you need to have a 50,000 square feet facility or larger. The storage facility I was looking at was only 25,000 square feet. What smaller facilities do is set up a system where it is self-service to the customer. Even with this system in place, someone still needs to be on call to show the spaces. I was also told that the small facilities lose some customers because there is not a person at the facility to help them right away.

For these reasons, the small self-storage facility should be in a strong market with a lot of apartments nearby. I had to walk away from this deal since the location was in a developing location with no apartments in the area. It can be frustrating to think you found a good property in which to invest and then, after spending a lot of time and energy, having to walk away. This is where a lot of people get frustrated with the entire process and stop looking for the right property.

Four Traits To Your Success

1. Perseverance and Dedication
2. Communication Skills
3. Passion
4. Knowledge of industry

1. PERSEVERANCE AND DEDICATION

Most important is perseverance and dedication, having the "do what it takes attitude" to become a success. When I started my Allstate insurance office, my motto was, failure is not an option. I actually took over an Allstate office that had failed.

That agent was intelligent and communicated effectively, but he was lazy. He did not have the perseverance and dedication to be successful. I had tried to help him and invited him to get involved with my dealership program. I wanted him to get involved in going to dealerships because, frankly, it can be a little intimidating going to dealerships on your own. Having two of us go into the dealership would have given me more confidence. He agreed, but every evening when we were supposed to meet, he backed out.

It was always the same excuse, "My wife wants me to go home for dinner."

I would tell him, "Dinner. Who cares about dinner? Eat later. We need to get to the dealerships to make some money."

He would always go home, and I would head to the dealerships. He failed, and I succeeded because of one thing. I had the perseverance and dedication to do what it takes to be a success.

Example: A friend was selling prescription drugs for Pfizer, earning approximately 90-100k per year. For most people that would be good; however, for my friend it was not good. He decided he wanted to work for a company that did a medical procedure during a heart by-pass operation. This company's procedure took veins from the leg to be used for the heart by-pass procedure.

My friend flew from Dallas to California to attend a national seminar with one goal in mind, to meet the owner of this particular company, give him a resume and set up an interview. Since there were thousands of people at this seminar, he printed out a picture of the owner and kept it in his pocket so the owner's image would be fresh in his mind. On the third and final day, my friend spotted the owner at the coffee station. He was able to have a small conversation with the owner and was able to set up an interview in a couple of weeks.

At the interview, my friend was told he had great communication skills. He had the knowledge and motivation to be a successful representative. There was just one point to be considered. My friend would need to be in the operating room, and there was a concern that all the blood from this invasive surgery might cause him to pass out during such a major procedure.

The owner raised the question, "How can I hire you if I do not even know how you would react to being in an operating room?"

My friend asked, "If I can be a witness to a heart by-pass operation in the next two weeks, will you give serious consideration to hiring me?"

The business owner agreed. My friend made it happen. A friend's mother was a nurse in the operating room in Atlanta, GA. He got approval from the surgeon and was off to Atlanta to view the surgery. Two weeks later he was hired, and his salary went up to $250,000 per year. This is a great example of perseverance and dedication.

Without this internal drive to succeed, whether it is in business, playing golf, or learning how to crochet, your perseverance and dedication to accomplish your goals is of utmost importance.

Many of the commercial property transactions and the title insurance business I am involved with took many months, and in some cases years, to bring together. These deals many times take a long time to put together because they have to be good for me. Obviously, I could put a deal together quickly; however, if it does not make financial success, why do the deal? If you believe in the new business, new property, or even new golf swing, you have to have the mental toughness to push forward no matter what happens.

Many times people get sidetracked by comments from family and friends and abandon their current project or goal. If negative comments bother you and affect your forward progress, stop telling these types of people your plans and goals. I can keep writing and writing, but perseverance comes down to your inner being and whether or not you will be resolute to make your goals happen.

2. COMMUNICATION SKILLS

Communication skills are the second most important attribute. Communication is the ability to get things done. You cannot be afraid to talk with people, ask questions and resolve problems. If you are afraid to talk on the phone, how will you get things done, how will you find answers to problems? If you are afraid or tentative to speak on the phone, start calling someone every day or three times per week. You get better at any task by practicing it often; this is true whether you want to be a better bowler, hair stylist, or communicator.

When I was an Allstate agent I spoke to people all day long for years. It is no accident that speaking on the phone is one of my best skills. If speaking is an issue for you, and I think it's an issue for 90% of the population, I recommend joining Toastmasters. This organization is an inexpensive and time effective way to improve your speaking skills. I recommend it and am currently a member.

Good communicators can get other people to see their point of view and then get them to go along with it. Many times an issue or topic will have two points of view. As an excellent communicator you will be able to effectively explain why your view makes the most sense.

I am currently speaking with a tenant regarding a lease renewal and small increase in rent. The tenant is adamant that he is paying enough already. He is threatening to move and overall does not want to discuss the issue. As an effective communicator, while speaking to the tenant I am going to remain calm and speak clearly and concisely to explain why the rent payments I am requesting are still a good deal in the local market. I will also explain how our company is customer service oriented, and how we work hard to maintain our properties at a high level.

3. PASSION

What are your goals in life, what do you enjoy doing? Many people I know really do not enjoy what they are doing. They would rather be doing something else the 40 or 50 hours a week they are at work. No matter what your passion is or what your interests are, you can start working toward your goals. No, it would not make sense to quit your job tomorrow to play video games or play basketball all day at the park. Nevertheless, you could start taking classes to be a video game programmer or start working up plans to start your own neighborhood youth basketball league.

My neighbor is really into soccer, so he started a recreational youth soccer league about 15 years ago. It has been a joy for him to operate since this is where his interest lies (his passion), and it has been a big positive for the community.

My passion once I was out of college was to make as much money as possible. It took many years to accomplish this goal, but I started working on it right out of college. The first thing I did was to enroll in a college to get a master's degree with a major in finance. I wanted to learn as much as possible about how the business and financial markets worked. The career paths I chose were based on the fact that I thought I could make a lot of money.

For example, I observed that a local wedding photographer made a lot of money. Soon after, I started a wedding videography business.

Another example is that one day my mom, who was a teller at a bank, told me that a State Farm insurance agent was always coming into the branch to deposit large checks. Before long I started working towards becoming an Allstate insurance agent. The goal of becoming an Allstate insurance agent was accomplished two years later.

Through talking with people and personal observance over the years, I became convinced that owning commercial property was a path to financial freedom. After many years of research, personal initiative, and determination, I purchased my first commercial office building in 2004.

Was becoming an Allstate agent, starting a wedding videography business, or purchasing a commercial property easy? No it was not, but I made it happen. The reason for success in changing your career path is mostly personal determination.

I have a friend who hates his job. Every time I see him I ask how the job is going. His response is always the same. He wishes he could do something else because this job is not for him. I then ask what he is doing to find a new line of work, and the answer is always, "nothing yet".

My guess is that my friend will never make a change to his career path. He will continue to hate his job for the next twenty years until he retires. That is a fun way to live your life! It is just too difficult for my friend to make a change to his normal daily routine.   He does not have much personal determination. Remember, if you don't go after what you want, you will never have it.

Passion is useless if there is no action to pursue it. Most people can tell you their passion, but few people act on that passion. The goal is to match up your action (your job) with your passion.

I have talked to many people who are not enjoying their current job. I usually ask if they are looking for a change to a different job, and the answer is almost always no. I would like to ask each person why not?

It is amazing how many people continue along in a job position or career that they dislike or flat out hate. So the question is why do people do this? I believe there are two main reasons.

The first reason is that people are unmotivated or lazy. People have to be able to dig deep inside to find the motivation. No one can find it for them.

Sometimes people are forced to get motivated when they lose their job.

My personal motivation was to make money and to live a more comfortable life than when I was growing up. Also, you live only once, so you might as well live it to the best of your abilities. On your deathbed you do not want to have any regrets.

The second reason is that people are afraid of change. It is natural for people to be afraid of the unknown. They start "what- if-ing" possible future problems. My wife started "what-if-ing" my first commercial property transaction.

She would say, "What if all the tenants leave? What if you need a new roof? What if a tenant falls in the parking lot and sues us?"

My response was, "What if the world comes to an end tomorrow, and then we will not have to worry about any of this."

But, seriously, I told her if this was going to cause her too much stress I would not go forward with the property purchase.

My wife finally said, "Go ahead with the purchase, and I will not "what if" you anymore." She has upheld her promise, and now eight years later she has not "what-if-d" me on any other transaction.

The fact is that on these property transactions I do my homework (due diligence), so I am making decisions based on extensive research. When the research steers me to purchase a property or business, I go forward with the transaction and do not change my mind because I get scared, worried or for any other emotional reason.

4. KNOWLEDGE OF INDUSTRY

It is important to become as knowledgeable as possible in the business you are about to start. Take advantage of other people's expertise, including the pitfalls they have encountered. Subscribe to magazines in your field, do online research, talk to other people currently in the business.

If the part about becoming knowledgeable in your field is a hassle or you find you are not interested, maybe this field or type of business is not your passion. Your expertise in your industry will expand rapidly once you have started your business. Yes, become as knowledgeable as possible, but do not let the fact that you are not an expert stop you from starting your business. People who want to be business owners sometimes think that others who already own businesses have some kind of hidden talent or gift. The fact is most people are about the same, and it comes down to perseverance and dedication, communication skills, passion, and knowledge of industry. These four characteristics will determine your success.

Allstate Agent

In 1995 I became an Allstate agent, but it was not easy. I interviewed three times with Allstate. The first two attempts failed because the Allstate representative who was supposed to meet with me did not even show up. After the third interview, Allstate decided to hire me, but first I had to take an internal Allstate test. The test was supposed to measure the likelihood I would be successful as an Allstate insurance agent. I took the test twice and failed both times.

Allstate then told me that I could not be hired as an Allstate insurance agent but could try again in one year. I could not understand how a company test was going to dictate my ability to be a successful agent. As this meeting ended, I stood up from the chair, said goodbye, and headed to the door of the office. I opened the door, walked out and was about to shut the door behind me when my brain said, do not give up yet.

Instead of leaving, I poked my head back inside the office and said, "I know I will be successful and you know I will be successful so there has to be something you can do to help me become an agent. I just cannot believe we are letting a computer program decide my future with this company."

She looked me in the eyes, there was silence, and I could see her brain was thinking. I then heard, "Take a seat. I may have another option for you."

I ended up working for an existing Allstate agent for six months. This would be a real world test, not a computer program, to determine if I could sell property and casualty insurance. I was now determined to prove the computer program wrong. Selling this type of insurance as a new agent is not an easy task. Most new agents fail. The company's idea of marketing is called tele-marketing, calling people out of the clear blue and trying to sell auto insurance. This method to me is a ridiculous waste of time and is very ineffective.

The most effective method I discovered was the auto dealership program. Why not go to a place where people needed auto insurance to drive off the lot and were actually interested in discussing insurance?

I had heard of a very successful agent about 10 miles away. In fact, he was the most successful agent in the region. My first question was how does this agent sell so much insurance? I was told he sold auto insurance at dealerships, but my territory supervisor told me this was not good insurance business and would be a bad idea for me to pursue. My underwriter told me there were a lot of claims with dealership business.

I was being advised against copying what the highest paid agent was doing. This made no sense to me. I was going through all the hard work of selling insurance to make a lot of money. Why else would I sell insurance? It is not fun or particularly rewarding. So I followed someone else's successes and set up my own auto dealership insurance program.

I did not have to think up an entire new sales strategy or re-invent the wheel. I basically copied another person's successful strategy and tried to make it better.

The dealership program became very successful; I became one of the most successful new agents for the company. Basically the way it worked was when a salesperson at a dealership needed auto insurance for a new or used car sale, he called me. I would jump in my car, drive to the dealership, and sell a new auto insurance policy on the spot. The salesperson sold the car right away before the customer started having second thoughts, and I sold a new insurance policy.

I also brought the dealerships pizza for lunch once per week. The important thing about the pizza is that I did not just drop it off and leave; I sat down and ate lunch with the sales staff each and every week. I not only became the guy who sold insurance, I also became friends with everyone in the dealership. The key is that I developed personal relationships with the sales staff. Within a couple of years it got to the point where I was eating pizza for lunch two or three times per day.

I also brought the female salespeople large chocolate bars. You would have thought I was bringing them bars of gold instead of bars of chocolate with all the excitement created when I walked in with the chocolate.

Because personal relationships were built with the auto dealerships and the food deliveries were constant, I had no worries that a competitor would swoop in and steal my business. I was able to prove that the Allstate computer program was not so smart in deciding who would be a successful insurance agent. Personal initiative and determination were the key attributes to success. I was determined from day one. Failure as an Allstate agent was not an option. This is the attitude that a new business owner must have.

AB Creative Videography

Most of my business ventures usually occur by observing other successful businesses. One does not have to reinvent the wheel to be successful, and in many cases you can actually copy a business. My dad's friend did wedding photography as a side business. It was well known that he made quite a bit of money on this side business, probably four or five times more than from his day job. This reinforced the idea that owning your own business is the way to go. I thought this was an opportunity to start a weekend business and make some decent money.

After further research (due diligence), we decided to start a wedding videography business instead of a wedding photography business. Having little knowledge of the wedding business, it seemed to me there would be a lot more competition doing wedding photography as well as more stress over goofing up a couple's wedding pictures.

The stepson of my dad's friend worked for a wedding videography business and agreed to let us follow him around for two weddings. The information we gathered was priceless. In one evening of following around a professional wedding videographer I had learned enough to get our business started.

This philosophy can be applied in other fields. If you want to open a coffee shop, go work at Starbucks for a month. Work at a hair salon for a month if you want to open a hair salon. Learn as much as you can about how the business operates. You do not need to tell your employer that your motive is to open a coffee shop or hair salon down the street.

Did I know everything about wedding videography at this time? Of course not, but I would learn along the way. Many people never start a business because they keep researching and researching about the industry and waiting for a planet to align with Jupiter. Often, too much research causes confusion and second guessing. I am not a big fan of creating a business plan. A business plan contains too many made up variables and takes too much time to complete. Am I saying to blindly start a business? Of course not.

After all the comments of family and friends that we could not and should not start the business, I pushed forward and started the business. I used all the money we had received from our own wedding one year earlier, about $4,000, to purchase video equipment. This left me with video equipment, no money in the bank and no customers. Now what? At the time, the internet was too new and of no help.

We became familiar with the wedding industry in the Detroit, MI area. We put a table up at a Target event that was free. This is where we found our first customer without spending any money on advertising. We agreed to videotape the wedding for $500, which was a low price even back in 1995. We had to start somewhere, and this first job started things rolling. I thought if we could get a few jobs and get our names out there things would take off.

The business did take off, mostly through word of mouth, and we were doing 35 weddings a year at about $1200 per wedding in our third year in business. Pretty good for a part-time weekend business. It was not luck that made the business successful; it was providing good service and a good product at a good price. As simple as that! This successful business came about by doing my homework on the business (due diligence) and then going ahead and starting the business even though I was told by many not to do it.

College professor?

Many times accomplishing things in life is not because you're the best or necessarily deserve something. It often comes down to perseverance. In 1995 I wanted to become a college professor. My first thought was, how will I accomplish this task? I applied for a few positions that I saw in the industry magazine, *The Chronicles of Higher Education*. These applications went nowhere; there were probably 500 people applying for each of the openings.

Yes, I had a Master's Degree in Finance but no doctorate degree and no teaching experience. Prospects were not looking good. How could I get in the front door? Every Sunday I looked through the employment classified ads for job openings to keep in touch with what was happening in the job market even though I was not looking for a job. One Sunday I noticed a small three line notice advertising a teaching position at a local college. I called the number, and the Dean of Business agreed that I could come in for an interview. At the interview I was told the school was looking for an English and computer instructor.

My Master's Degree in Finance would not work. I thanked the dean for the interview and walked out the door.

Was I done pursuing a teaching position at this college? NO WAY! Every month, without fail, I went back to speak with the dean. I wanted to show my commitment to teaching at the college. Did I call ahead of time? No. The dean would have had nothing new to say, if I could have spoken with him at all. When I walked in the front door someone had to speak with me, and usually it was the dean.

Month after month I made the 30-minute trek to the college to attempt to talk with the dean. I continued to be turned down. By the fourth visit we were becoming friends, that is the dean and me. He started smiling when he saw me. I know he was thinking, are you here again, you never give up.

On the eighth visit I was finally hired. Was I the most qualified? Of course not. Nonetheless, the most persistent person, me, was offered the job. I was now a college professor. On the visit when I was offered the position, I walked into the dean's office and was asked to take a seat. That was a good sign which had not happened before. The dean and I made some small talk for a few minutes before he opened his desk and pulled out a thick folder and started looking through it. There was silence at this point. Was he pulling out a restraining order so I would stop bothering him?

Finally he looked up at me and asked, "Would you teach English?"

I said, "That is about the only class I would decline."

"How about teaching computers?" he asked.

"I will do it!" I thanked him for the opportunity.

As I was walking out the dean said, "By the way, what kind of degree do you have?"

"Finance," I responded.

I was so persistent that I was hired, having only a finance degree, to teach a computer class. I had very little computer background to qualify me to teach computers but thought I could figure it out, and I did.

About one year into teaching at this college, the dean asked if I could help teach an extra computer class, Word Perfect to be exact. I agreed. On the first day of class I began to teach Word Perfect.

Twenty minutes into the class a student raised his hand and proclaimed, "This class is not Word Perfect. It is Microsoft Word."

The dean had accidently given me the incorrect information. So there I was, suddenly standing in front of 40 students and having no knowledge of Microsoft Word. In fact, I had never even used it. Many of the students probably knew more about Microsoft Word than I, but I was supposed to teach the class.

It was at this point I told the class, "We are going to take a 20 minute break."

I then rushed to the bookstore to get the teacher's manual, sat down, and tried to figure out what I was doing. I made it through the first class, and by the end of the semester I was an expert in Microsoft Word.

Golf Course

In 2000, it became obvious that my career at Allstate was coming to an end. The company began raising premiums on the insurance policies anywhere from 25 to 75 percent and began putting heavy pressure on the agents to sell disability insurance. I did not mind the price increases if the company would have allowed us to sell insurance through other companies at the same time. Many customers were leaving my agency because of the exorbitant price increases. At this same time the territory manager was telling me I had to sell a large amount of disability insurance, or I would be fired. It was then that I realized I needed to apply my perseverance and determination to another venture. I began to come up with my next plan.

I initially wanted to purchase a golf course and get out of the insurance business. I found several brokers who only dealt with golf courses and started researching every golf course that was for sale east of the Mississippi River. After about two months I was beginning to figure out the type of golf course that I thought would be profitable and fit within my budget. If the opportunity arose, I would contact the owners of the golf course and ask them every question I could think of. I was quickly gaining knowledge of the industry; doing my due diligence.

At this point I started visiting golf courses in person to ask more questions and to possibly consider an offer if I liked what I saw. Sometimes I would show up early, like a day early, to look at the golf course so the owner could not cover up anything before my scheduled arrival.

One particular incident comes to mind. A golf course went up for sale on the east side of Charlotte, North Carolina on a Thursday morning. Since I had been studying golf courses that were for sale over the last several months, I knew that this type of course was what I was looking for. So I had to look at the course, pronto. If it was a good deal, it would be sold quickly.

At about 1:00 pm on Friday, I jumped into my Honda Accord with Mark, my 16 year old brother-in-law, to make the trip to see the golf course. By Friday night we made it to somewhere in Kentucky from Detroit, MI. We decided to get a hotel room and continue our journey in the morning. The next day we left at 8:00 am and finally arrived at the golf course at 4:30 pm. When we arrived at the course, it was lightly raining, was beginning to get dark since it was the first week of December, and was about 40 degrees outside. The only car in the parking lot belonged to the manager of the club. He had been told by the owner to wait for us.

As I pulled into the parking lot, I rolled down the window and said, "Get us a cart, we are playing golf."

He thought I was kidding since it was cold, raining, and would be dark in about 1½ hours.

I said, "We just drove 800 miles, and we are playing golf and checking out this golf course!"

We played all 18 holes in the next 1½ hours in the rain and cold. The manager was still waiting for us when we finished. By this time he was not very happy, but I still asked him to show me around the clubhouse and every other building that was owned by the business.

By 8:00 pm I had done all of the due diligence I could handle for the day. Mark and I headed into downtown Charlotte to find a hotel for the night. On the way to the hotel, I received a call from my wife saying a huge snowstorm was on the way that evening, and we would most likely be stranded in Charlotte, North Carolina for two or three days. Instead of being stranded in Charlotte, we drove through the night back to Cleveland, OH and arrived at my brother's house at 5:30 am Sunday morning.

Why do I tell this story? To show what I would go through to purchase a golf course. This is the kind of dedication you will need to start a new business and be successful. Perseverance and dedication are required.

Did I purchase the golf course? No. The back nine of the course is a very poor setup. I would not have known this had I not played all eighteen holes in the cold, rainy weather. Also, the course was located too far out in the country. This course would be successful in a highly populated area. To convince golfers to drive 30 minutes, the golf course has to be worth the trip, and this course would not be worth the trip.

Evans Insurance

Evans Insurance was established in 1967, and the owner finally decided after 35 years he had enough and wanted to retire. I found the business for sale online and was negotiating the deal via the phone without actually seeing the business in person. Very bad idea which I would never do again. We agreed on the price, but the owner would not sign off until I met him in person. So the next day I left from Michigan to drive to Florida to talk with the owner and finalize the contract.

Looking back, I realize I did not do enough due diligence on this business. I was more concerned about moving to sunny Florida. The business was in more disarray than I thought; nonetheless, I was able to turn it around in six months. It took a lot, and I mean a lot, of work.

One year into this new venture I realized that the property and casualty business was no longer my passion. In 2003 a local Allstate agent walked in my office and stated he wanted to purchase the business. He knew the original owner and always wanted to purchase the business. After convincing me he was serious, I told him the price I would accept for my business. He said the price was good with him and that he would work on getting financing. Two weeks later he called to tell me that he could not find financing and that he did not have enough funds to pay cash.

I thought that this was the end of the deal. Six months later, however, on December 1, 2003, he called me on the phone to tell me he had found financing. The deal had to be closed by the end of the year so on the last business day of 2003 the paperwork was signed, at my full asking price of course. This was the end of my career in selling property and casualty insurance. It was successful in the fact that I now had enough money to move forward and start purchasing commercial properties.

Residential condo

It was 1996, my inside sales position was going no-where, and I decided to make my first move into real estate as an investment. After looking at a few properties I finally settled on purchasing a residential one-bedroom condo. At the time, I did not know what I was doing. The main reason I purchased the condo was that it was affordable and fit within my budget. In retrospect, this was not a good reason to purchase the property.

The property I found for sale was listed in the Sunday paper. I called about the ad and set up an appointment to look at the property the next day. The condo was in poor condition. An elderly lady had just passed away, and the son was now trying to sell. It needed new flooring throughout, new paint, and upgrades in the kitchen and bathroom. The owner was asking $39,000. I offered $32,000, and we settled on $35,000. Thinking back, I realize that I did not know what I was doing. I did not know if $35,000 was a good price or not. What I knew was that I wanted as low a price as possible. I was not a very good negotiator at this time since I had very little experience.

After the purchase I went ahead and updated the property. I did most of the work myself except for the new carpet. The carpet was so old it literally disintegrated as it was pulled up.

After calling local apartments to research rental rates, it appeared that $600 would be a fair price. An ad was placed in the paper. Remember, you're better off getting it leased to the right person rather than holding out for an extra $50 and then letting it sit vacant. I was able to find a single female about 25 years old who leased the condo the first year.

I started to receive calls from the condo association president telling me the condo association needed to interview any new tenant and give their approval before I could lease the space. I did not think too highly of this association rule and kept ignoring the phone calls from the association president. From a property owner standpoint, getting association approval to lease a space was too cumbersome a requirement. I basically ignored the association, and nothing came of it. The association could have enforced the repeated threats of fines by placing liens against the property. These are the kinds of problems you can run into while owning property within an association. Be very cautious of associations. Read the condo association rules very carefully before purchasing a property to use as a rental. I did not read the rules of the association before purchasing the property. **This was my mistake.**

The second tenant I leased to was an engaged couple (without association approval). They were IN LOVE (or they thought so), happy, and excited about their future. One month later I received a phone call from Pete.

"Hi Pete," I said. "How are the wedding plans going?"

He replied, "Susie is a blanking blank! She had an affair that I found out about last night so she left this morning for Tennessee, and I just moved out. Keep the security deposit. Have a nice life."

That was the end of the second tenant. I went to the property and it was a mess, but there was no damage. There were 12 black roses on the table. That seemed odd so I called Pete back and asked about the black roses. He said he left the 12 black roses to signify that she was dead to him. That love affair did not last long.

After cleaning up the condo, I decided to sell and stay focused on single family homes to purchase and lease out. I was also getting tired of the messages from the condo association saying that I was breaking the rules. The property ended up selling for $35,000, the same as the purchase price.

I did not make any money on the deal, but it was a great learning experience. Looking back on the deal, the most important thing was that I moved forward on the deal, did my best, and gained a lot of experience. Do not expect to know all the answers, especially on your first deal. If you want to know all of the answers you will never purchase anything.

Did you join the rat race?

You are a member of the rat race if you or your family continues to purchase bigger homes and nicer cars as your income increases. If your financial goals revolve around purchasing a bigger and more expensive home, you are not going down the path to financial independence. Why is it that people tend to work harder and harder to purchase larger homes, more expensive cars, in-ground pools, large gas grills, huge TV's, etc.? In the process of working harder and trying to get that next promotion, they are actually causing more personal stress, usually spending less time with family, and paying more income tax along the way.

Your home is not an asset because it does not generate positive cash flow; in fact, it only creates expense.

As one purchases a larger home, the property tax, insurance, electric bill, and maintenance costs all increase. I would still recommend a house over an apartment as long as you will live there more than two years because it will, over time, increase in value. Instead of purchasing a bigger home or building the new pool, use the money from the increased value of your home to purchase an asset.

To repeat, assets include businesses, properties, or some type of royalties. This new asset will generate more cash for your everyday life. The bigger home only creates greater expenses. If you want to purchase a bigger home, that is ok; however, please do not call it an investment.

About two years ago I purchased a small strip center instead of buying a pool, a new car, or bigger house. I spent $150,000 to purchase the strip center. The strip center gave me an additional $30,000 in positive cash flow per year.

As you acquire more properties and other assets, you will begin to enjoy receiving the monthly checks. They keep arriving month after month. But sometimes the checks do not arrive; then what do you do? I recommend setting up a normal process to use for all the tenants. In other words, treat all tenants the same.

My tenants' lease payments are due the first day of each month. If a lease payment is not received by the 10th day of the month, a $100 late fee is assessed. If the payment is not received by the 10th day, I start calling the tenant to ask if he has mailed out the lease payment. Usually the tenant just forgot, and it was no big deal. I continue to call every three or four days until the lease payment is received. If the payment is not received by the 25th day of the month, I start the eviction process. Many property owners let tenants get several months behind; tenants will not get caught up once they get 30 days past due. There are exceptions, of course. Sometimes there is an out of the ordinary circumstance such as the tenant being in the hospital or on vacation.

Do not start driving around to pick up lease payments; your time is more valuable than that. It is the tenants' responsibility to get their lease payments to you. I do **not** give out my home address to tenants if they want to send payments overnight. I am sure they could find out where I live if they wanted, but I feel better thinking they do not know where I live. I tell them to send their payments by normal mail, and as long as they are postmarked by the 10th day of the month there is no late fee. Enforce the late fee if you want tenants to take you seriously about paying lease payments on time.

I recently acquired a lease through a property I just purchased, and the late fee was $60 per day starting on the 5th day of the month. The first month the tenant paid 15 days late, but since I was the new owner I decided that it would be fair to give the tenant a break and not charge a late fee. I sent an email and followed up with a phone call explaining that starting next month we would be enforcing the late fee of $60 per day after the 5th day of the month. Sure enough, the following month I received the tenant's lease payment 10 days late. I called the tenant to explain that I could not accept the payment without the late fee and until the late fee was sent, another $60 per day would have to be added for the late fee. Needless to say, the tenant was not very happy to pay an additional $300. Since enforcing the late fee this one month, I have received the payment on time every month.

How much to charge

When you are the landlord, making the most money is your goal. I have found that making the most money means keeping your spaces full and giving the tenants a good value for their money. The first thing that I do to keep tenants is to keep the property well maintained. This is an ongoing weekly process. A property will quickly go into disarray if you ignore it. Tenants notice a neglected property and will start looking for a new place to lease. Tenants want a professional, well-kept environment for their customers and employees. Secondly, I tend to keep my tenants lease rates about five to ten percent below market rates. **Keeping your spaces full is your most important goal**. Do not neglect the asset that pays you each and every month.

Property Problems

Your property is a business, and problems will arise. Develop a list of reliable contractors to call when you have a problem. Get to know one or two handymen who can take care of incidental issues that arise. Problems will range from the most trivial to the most major. Some tenants will consider it a crisis, no matter what the issue, and will call you in a panic. The most important thing is to remain calm and level headed. Gather all the information about the issue, evaluate it, resolve the problem, and then move on.

Here is an incident that arose a few weeks ago. A young adult, about 19 years old, started sitting outside a business several hours a day to get free wifi (internet). The tenant next door became involved in a heated argument with this person. The tenant then called the police about the issue. Next, he called me to let me know his customers were scared of this person. He and his wife were also afraid because they believed this young person to be a criminal. He wanted me to file a police report or get a restraining order. I listened to all of his comments and told the tenant I understood his concerns. I asked him to let me make some phone calls and figure out the best resolution. In the meantime, I suggested that he try to relax and not speak with this person no matter what.

To resolve the issue, I contacted the tenant who was providing the free wifi and told him he had to secure the wifi with a password to prevent this person from hanging out at the property. The wifi was secured with a password by the next day. We never saw the young adult again, and the problem was easily resolved. I did not have to file a police report or hire a security guard which could have potentially escalated the problem. **Think** before you react, and most times it is a simple and quick resolution.

A friend of mine named Steve called me after getting back from a skiing vacation. Steve and his wife were thinking about purchasing a condo near the ski resort to use as a rental property. He asked me if it was a good idea.

I asked, "Is your primary reason to enjoy the condo on vacation or to try and make money?"

The response was that they would like to try and make some money.

"Then I would not do it," I responded. "You cannot manage a property 2000 miles away, so you would need a management company. They could easily take 40 to 50 percent of the income. Next, the condo is in a seasonal area so six months or more of the year it will sit empty. Also, no one can predict how much it will be worth in five years. It could be worth a lot less. On the other hand, if you want to purchase the condo for your personal enjoyment, then go for it."

Residential vs Commercial

Investing in commercial real estate is much more profitable than residential real estate. Commercial properties are also much easier to manage. The commercial tenant will be a business owner who wants to take care of the property because that is where he earns his money. Many times the residential tenant has the attitude that this is not my house and I am only going to live here one or two years so who cares what happens to this house. It is much easier to evict commercial tenants as opposed to residential tenants, as my story below will show.

Let's also consider the property maintenance issue with residential and commercial properties. In a home you are renting out, you have one tenant paying monthly rent. With this one tenant in this one home, you have to be concerned about the one roof. In a commercial property you could have ten tenants under one roof. When involved in residential investing, to have ten tenants you would need ten houses with ten roofs. That is a lot of roofs to maintain, repair, or replace.

I have a friend who has about 40 residential homes which he leases out. He had to hire two full-time employees to keep up with making repairs, getting new tenants, or evicting tenants who stopped paying their rent. With 40 commercial rentals, you could easily manage it on your own.

If you still want to have residential rental properties, here is one strategy for a young investor that I used twenty years ago. First, you purchase a home to live in. After moving in you start looking for another home to purchase. When you find a second home to purchase, tell the bank you will be moving into this second house so you can get a regular home loan. You **do** move into this second home. You will rent out your first home, but you don't need to tell the bank that.

If you were trying to get a loan for an investment property, it would be much more difficult than getting a regular home loan. The interest rate would be higher on an investment loan, and you would have to put a lot more money down.

After purchasing the second home, go out and purchase a third home and follow the same process. So, after the third home purchase, you have two rental properties and live in the third home. You will have three home loans as if you lived in each home. The bank could force you to get an investment loan if they ever found out you were not living in the house; however, that will not happen because you pay your bills on time each month. This is a quick way to get residential investment properties.

With a residential investment property you want to look for a house under $150,000 in a stable area with good public schools. The home that you purchase should be a standard type of house that fits in with the neighborhood. Do not purchase the odd-ball house. We looked for ranch houses that had three bedrooms and 1½ or 2 full bathrooms. This is the type of house that a young couple with one child would like to rent.

We had a residential rental house in Michigan, and the tenants stopped paying their rent. They had an option to purchase the home for $125,000. We made the mistake of listening to their excuses for six months before we took action to start the eviction process. We filed the wrong paperwork at first, and it took two more months to figure that out. We now had not received a rent payment in six months. Since we were inexperienced with evictions, we hired an attorney to get the deadbeat tenants evicted. Three months later we received the court ruling that the tenant must vacate the premises. By this time we hadn't received rent in ten months.

Someone from the Sheriff's Office went to the house to give the tenants notice that they had two days to vacate. The Sheriff agreed to meet me at the house two days later to make sure that they had vacated the house so I would not be walking into the house alone to face an angry tenant. When the Sheriff and I walked in we saw that they had, in fact, left but had destroyed the house. There was damage to the walls, missing fixtures, broken glass and clothing strewn throughout the house. They had also ripped up and taken all of the landscaping from the front yard. In two weeks, at a cost of $10,000, we were able to bring the house back to good condition. We had the last laugh, though. We ended up putting the property on the market and sold it for $148,000. That is $23,000 more than we were going to sell it to the renters who had the option to purchase.

New railing to prevent lawsuit

Taking proper care of your property will also serve you well in the event of a lawsuit. Quickly resolve any issues that could lead to injury at every property. Even though an injury can happen anywhere, you do not want it to happen due to your negligence. Here is a recent example of extra caution I decided to take at a property.

This particular property has a 70 foot handicap ramp. The existing railing was designed for residential use, not for an outdoor commercial application. The existing railing also had several cracks since it was made of wood. If someone were to fall and injure himself due to the railing, I would be liable. It was not the correct railing even though it was a railing. To resolve the issue I installed an aluminum commercial grade railing. See pictures.

Aluminum does not rust so the railing should last a long time. Someone can still fall on the ramp, but it will not be because I was lazy and did not install the proper railing.

Get creative

Negotiations for commercial properties can be as creative as you want to make them. There are no set rules, what you agree to is what you agree to. Most sellers want their money right away, but once in a while they may agree to act like the bank and finance the deal. **One mistake I have seen buyers make is paying too much for a property just because the seller is willing to finance the deal when the bank would not do the financing**. Do not pay too much for a property regardless of the financing.

If a lender does not want to finance a property, maybe there is a good reason. Sometimes, though, there may not be a good reason. I have been turned down many times by lenders over the years but eventually found financing, and the properties have been very profitable. My first commercial property took five trips to lenders before a local community bank finally said yes. The local community banks will be your best choice if you are new to commercial real estate.

One time a negotiation for a $1,000,000 property was at a standstill. I was offering $1,000,000, and the seller would not go below $1,100,000 no matter what. At least that is what he said. I found out the seller liked BMW cars, so I offered $1,000,000 plus a BMW. The BMW would cost me an additional $40,000. The seller did not accept my offer with the BMW, but I think I proved that I was serious because shortly thereafter he agreed to $1,050,000.

Property for sale

Here is a listing I saw on loopnet.com.

Coldwell Banker ███████   ███████████

Retail Property For Sale

Clermont Highway 50 location 4 unit strip center

███████████ FL 34711

Price:	$550,000
Gross Leasable Area:	3,840 *SF*
Price/SF:	$143.23
Property Type:	Retail
Property Sub-type:	Strip Center
Additional Sub-types:	Office Building
	Street Retail
Property Use Type:	Investment
Commission Split:	3%
No. Stories:	1
Tenancy:	Multiple
Year Built:	1987
Lot Size:	0.38 *AC*
APN / Parcel ID:	███████
Listing ID	19373626
Last Updated	8 days ago

Find Out More.

Highlights

- 4 units, mixed use as retail and office now
- One unit vacant - perfect for owner-occupant
- Zoned for preofessional office, retail can even be converted to Office condos
- City of Clermont welcomes new businesses and growth
- Aerial video also available
- Blocks from downtown Clermont and new redevelopment of waterfront park areas.

Description

Fantastic Highway 50 frontage in growing Clermont, even nearer to downtown redevelopment area up and coming. 4 units, 22 shared parking spaces, signage and frontage on Highway 50.

Approx 1000SF per unit. One long term tenant, one vacancy for easy show, or owner occupant to move into it and retain rest as investment. Additional aerial photos and video available.

Clermont, FL

Map of ▓▓▓▓▓▓▓▓▓▓▓▓ Clermont, FL 34711 (Lake County)

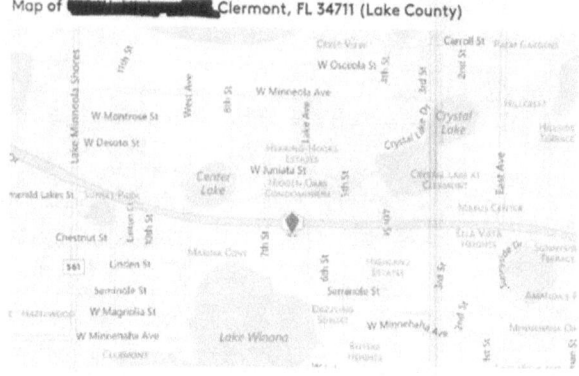

Since this property was in a good location and the spaces were a good size, it warranted a call to the listing real estate agent to get more info. I found out the property had city water and city sewer, which is good. I found out that three spaces were leased at $1200 per month each, and one space was vacant.

The broker tried to tell me that the vacant space could be leased for $1500 per month and the other tenants were paying below market rent because the owner didn't want to rock the boat and increase rents. He also said that checking other vacant spaces in the immediate area would give me a better idea of what rental rates were per square foot.

I told the broker that I may be able to get $1500 for the vacant space but for my calculations to determine an offer I had to go with what the other spaces are leasing for each month. That amount was $1200.

This property was built in 1987. I like properties built after 1979 because that is the year asbestos was banned and the year they stopped manufacturing it. I would purchase a property built before 1979, but it is always a positive if the property was built after that year. Asbestos has to be professionally removed, and this process can be expensive. I have found asbestos to be a problem in older buildings that have popcorn ceilings. If older than 1979, the odds are the popcorn ceiling was made with asbestos.

The roof was 10 years old, and there was adequate parking. There were 22 parking spaces, or 5 ½ spaces per 1000 square feet. Do not go below four spaces per 1000 square feet or you may get into parking issues.

Let me summarize how I arrived at my offer. Four units each rented @ $1200 per month or $57,600 per year. I figured the property taxes, property insurance, electric, water, repairs and reserves would amount to roughly $17,000 leaving a net profit before taxes of $40,000. I believed the market price to be 10 times $40,000 which is $400,000. This would be a 10 cap.

I emailed a letter of intent explaining how I arrived at an offer of $400,000 and stating that I believed this to be the fair market value. I was not expecting the seller to accept since the asking price was $550,000 and the property had just gone on the market. There was no response from the seller, and I had to call the broker directly two days later to verify she had received my offer after my many text messages were not returned.

The broker informed me that the seller was not interested in selling for $400,000 or any price near that.

"Not a problem," I said. "I understand, and the seller can sell for whatever price he wants. If the seller changes his mind, I would welcome a counter offer to keep the conversation going."

The seller would not counter.

This is a typical situation where the seller thinks the property is worth more than it is. I will follow up every few weeks or so to continue developing a relationship with broker and seller. I have been in these situations many times before and have usually ended up purchasing the property even if it takes one to three years.

Parking Issues

Nothing gets a tenant more upset than the tenant not having a place to park or other tenants parking in front of other businesses. A tenant just called me the other day while I was on vacation. He was upset that another business owner was parking in front of his business, stating that it was not fair and that he was going to lose customers. Was the tenant exaggerating? Yes, but I agree that the spaces in front of his business should be left open for customers.

I could have just waited until I made it home from vacation but decided to call the customer (tenant) right away to let him know that I understood his concern and to tell him that I was out of town but would get the situation corrected as soon as I got back into town. The tenant was happy that I was concerned and was calmed down. If I had not called, he would have continued to become more upset, started spreading the word around that the landlord does not care about his business, and may have gotten into a verbal argument with the other business owner who was parking in his space.

After getting back home I was able to figure out who was parking in his space. It was a new employee of another business, and she did not realize what she was doing. The problem was quickly resolved.

Always put in your lease the maximum parking spaces each business can use. In this case the maximum would be five. Also, I always tell the tenant that I am not going to be standing in the parking lot trying to enforce these rules; nonetheless, if parking problems do start happening, at least I have it in the lease to enforce.

I had a property management company years ago that decided to start doing telemarketing work. They packed 15 people into an 1100 square foot space. The parking situation was instantly a problem, and every tenant was upset with me. I did not know what to do or even if I could do anything because I had nothing in the lease which covered the allowed parking spaces per tenant. I lost one good tenant over the issue and was lucky that the tenant causing the problem moved out quickly thereafter.

Commercial brokers

Commercial real estate agents can be a good source to find leads. Developing long term relationships with several commercial brokers will help you find the right deal. Just remember, they are into making the deal close. Sometimes they turn into cheerleaders trying to get the deal to the finish line even when sometimes your best interest is to step back and not do the deal.

Sales agents are good at selling. Most of them do not own any property themselves and do not even know what would make a great rental property. After closing the property will be yours, and the real estate agent will not be concerned or responsible for any issues concerning the property. Heck, you may never see the real estate agent again. Take advice from a broker with a grain of salt. In other words, do not believe a broker until you can verify the information.

Convenience store

Next to one of my properties is a small rundown convenience store. The convenience store is just about to go out of business since the WaWa was built next door. About the day the WaWa convenience store opened, the property went up for sale. The asking price was $400,000. I knew the area was good, and the property had good potential. I figured it would cost about $50,000 in renovations to get the property in the condition I wanted. My first offer was $250,000. I did not just make the number up. I knew the rent or cash flow I could generate from the property and, after considering the $50,000 in renovations, determined that $250,000 was a fair price and a good deal for me. After six months of going back and forth on price, we could not come to an agreement. My last offer was $350,000 which was over market value, but I figured it would still be a good deal since I already had a tenant lined up for the space. A few days after this I was looking at the property appraiser website and decided to take a look at the convenience store property on-line. To my surprise the listed owner was not the same person from whom I was trying to buy the property.

I called the person I had been negotiating with for the last six months and asked, "Do you own the property?"

The answer was no. He then said the owner had asked him to find a buyer. I said that I now understood but did not want to discuss this further because I was not too happy at this moment and did not want to get into an argument. But I was thinking, at no time over the last six months did you not think it would be appropriate to tell me that you did not own the property?

After a little work and help from my real estate agent friend, I was able to find the name and phone number of the real owner. I called the owner and found out he lived 1000 miles away from the property and wanted to sell. He told me he wanted $400,000.00. I told him my best offer was $300,000.00 and the reasons why, including the $50,000.00 in renovations. He asked me to email him with my best offer in the next few days. I said I could email him an offer, but it would be the same offer I was verbally telling him. He said okay. A few days later I emailed him and offered $300,000.00. He said he had thought about it a little more and now wanted $500,000.00. I told him I was still at $300,000.00 and gave you my best offer right away.

It has now been six months since this email conversation. There has been no response. I will eventually buy this property because no one is going to pay more than $300,000.00. Sometimes it takes many months or years for the owner to come to grips with the market value of his property. I learned to verify whether or not I was speaking with the owner before trying to purchase a property.

Do not make decisions based on the tax code

The current Federal tax code is ridiculous. I call it "Government Gone Wild". My accountant recently told me that if I tried my best to follow each rule of the tax code I still would not be able to do it because the code has gotten too confusing and ridiculous. Make investment decisions on the validity of how good the investment is, **not on possible tax consequences**. If you hold an investment property for longer than one year before selling, you pay a much lower rate of 15% on the income earned. It is not a surprise that the fastest growing regions of the country are in the states with no state income tax.

Massive tax write-off on commercial properties

There are massive write-offs on commercial property. I have not owed Federal income tax in five years due to the massive tax benefits of owning commercial property. This is definitely a large advantage of owning commercial property. The system of having large tax write-offs for property owners was set up by the Federal government to encourage more investment in property. With the increase in property ownership, it is easier for low income households to find affordable places to live. I wish the Federal Government would switch to a flat tax or fair tax and get rid of all these loopholes even though this loophole benefits me greatly.

Business plans over rated

Too many unknown variables go into forecasting a business plan. The business plan becomes a guesstimate into future years. I would either recommend passing on the business plan or just putting together some basic thoughts. The most important thing is putting your good idea into action. Get the business going. When I say get the business going, this does not mean you have to quit your job right away or spend a lot of money. Moving forward cautiously is okay. Most people do the "cautious" part but never do the "move forward" part.

Refinance to get cash out

My normal advice is, don't sell your commercial property investment. If the property was good enough when you purchased it, most likely it is still good enough today. But if the property has increased in value and you want to get the money out of it, what do you do? If you sell the property, you have to pay capital gains taxes and you no longer own the property. What you want to do is refinance the property and pull the money out tax free. You still own the property.

Hewlett Packard 12B
(Business Calculator)

It is imperative that you become familiar with using a business calculator. How are you going to know what your monthly payment will be on a business, property, or car purchase? It is not hard to learn how to use these calculators. The owner's manual is very easy to understand. There are five variables, and you will need information on three of these variables to make a calculation.

Save as much money as possible as quickly as possible. This could mean working extra hours, a second job, or maybe doing without cable until you have saved $50,000. Where do I put the money as I am saving it? Stock market, mutual funds, gold, silver, bonds, options, futures contracts, under mattress, savings – all are available options.

This money should go into a federally insured savings account. The online accounts work well, with better interest than the local neighborhood banks. Go to Bankrate.com to find the best deal.

The main goal here is to save money to purchase an asset. An asset, again, is something that earns money, unlike the home you live in. Gold and silver do not earn you any money; they just sit in a safe deposit box. A bond will earn you money, but if interest rates go up, your bond is now worth less if you want to sell it. Concerning mutual funds, we hear all the time that we should invest for the long term. Investment companies say over a 10, 20, or 30 year period you are likely to earn 10, 12, or 15% per year. I wonder what 10, 20, or 30 year period they are talking about. I have had mutual funds for many decades. The value never seems to change much. My wife put $50,000 in an IRA about 10 years ago, and it was invested into an S&P 500 index mutual fund. The value is about the same today. I am not sold on the mantra, invest for the long term. How long is long term? I know it is too long for me.

You have now saved your $50,000 or whatever sum of money you set as your goal, and you have also paid down your debt (hopefully). I said hopefully paid down your debt also, because this affects your credit score. Your credit score needs to be above 700. You can go to annualcreditreport.com once a year and get your score for free. Basically, what you need to do is <u>pay your bills on time, all the time</u>. Do not worry about all the reasons your credit score will fluctuate. I repeat, just <u>pay your bills on time, all the time</u>, and your score will steadily improve.

Make it happen

Making it happen comes down to you. Do you have what it takes to operate a successful business or purchase an apartment building?

In 1995, I was working an inside sales position that paid $18,000 per year and was going nowhere. There was no chance of promotion or excelling in this small business. I volunteered to do outside sales, but the owner was not interested. I learned many things at this business, the first being that some business owners can be flat out liars.

I was told when I started that a small portion of the company's annual earnings would be invested each year in my personal 401k plan. I understand that things change and there are no guarantees so was not too upset when I was told after year one that this benefit was now being discontinued. Three years later, however, I found out that the other three employees continued to get contributions to their 401k plans even though I was told by the owner that the company had discontinued that benefit.

When I questioned the owner, he said, "Too bad. I am the owner and will do what I want."

Also, I was a part-time prisoner of the company. I had to arrive at 8:00 am sharp each and every day and could not leave the prison grounds until 5:00 pm. I learned very quickly that I did not want to keep working for this owner or any other company. I became very motivated at this point to become my own boss.

But what kind of company should I start or possibly purchase? That was a tough question. There are two ways to make money; you physically work and earn a certain amount per hour, this applies to salaried employees also, or you have your money work for you. I, personally, enjoy having my money work for me instead of having to be at a job every day.

Where do I put my money to work? Traditional places like savings accounts, bonds, and mutual funds will not work unless you are worth more than ten million dollars. To make it work, your money has to own assets. This could include property, businesses, a book you wrote, partial ownership in an oil well, or a right to any asset that earns money. Once this is accomplished, you will be earning money without having to personally work. This is called passive income; you don't have to actually work to earn money.

Currently I am earning enough passive income so I can get out of bed whenever I want. One of my neighbors used to consistently ask me if I had won the lottery because she always saw me walking my dog in the middle of the day while most people were at work. This person thinks the only way to make a living is to actually go to work. I repeatedly told my neighbor that I did not win the lottery, and I know she was always wondering about how I could pay my bills.

Being a landlord

My first comment is that when a contractor completes a job and it is done correctly, pay him right away. Why not? If you owe it, pay it. Contractors remember this, and the next time you need their help they will go to your job before someone who does not pay in a timely manner. You may also get a little better pricing because it is a huge hassle for contractors when they have to track down deadbeats who do not pay.

Keeping your properties maintained can give you a huge advantage over other property owners, especially owners who use management companies. These property owners tend to turn the property over to the management company and then forget about it. If they manage on their own, most do not actively keep things maintained. Management companies also cut into your profits.

I would recommend that as things break you fix them right away. If you turn a blind eye to problems, eventually your property will become run down and become an eyesore. A dilapidated property is harder to rent out and gives tenants an easier reason to leave. Take care of your asset, and it will take care of you. And, again, why is something an asset? It is an asset because it earns you money.

The main reason to manage your commercial property yourself is because it is easy. Also, you can respond faster to tenant problems and avoid some tenants leaving over issues that can be resolved.

A common issue with a tenant is the space becoming too small; his business has grown. Sometimes you can reconfigure the space. Take down a wall, add a wall, be creative, and do what it takes to keep the tenant. Many times I have had tenants move to larger spaces within the same complex or something I own nearby. If tenants say it's a pain to move, tell them you will pay for the move. If a tenant still needs to leave, be gracious and thank them for renting the space. They will see when they move to their new space how good they had it when they rented from you. They may be your tenants again in the future, so do not burn any bridges.

It's about the customer

Keeping your customers happy should be your first objective. Without customers or tenants, there is no business. Make sure they stay happy so they will continue patronizing your business. At the title insurance office this is the most important thing we do each day. Our customers know that if there is a question or problem regarding their closing, they can call us directly and we will solve the problem. We have Customer Appreciation parties twice per year to thank our customers for their business.

I try to keep the rental properties maintained and updated so the tenants feel they are receiving a good value for their monthly lease payment. I also give the tenants my personal cell phone number in case of an emergency. Sometimes a customer can push you or your business so far that this particular customer turns into a liability. This type of customer might be constantly calling you for irrelevant issues or consuming a large amount of your time without actually providing much income to your business. These are the customers you want to get rid of; they are doing harm to your business. So, yes, you want to take care of your customers except for the few who cause you all the grief.

First of all, I always intend to follow all government rules. I pay my property taxes on time as well as all the other government fees that I am assessed. There are times when the local government gets so ridiculous with the permits that it may be advantageous to consider doing a job without the permit. Some of the times to consider avoiding permits would include: replacing electrical outlets, removing small walls, flooring, minor plumbing, and fences.

Recently at an office building, I was required by the city to install not only one but two drinking fountains.

Why two? One for the handicapped and one for the standing people even though the drinking fountain for the handicapped was only two inches lower than the other fountain. Why the government requires even one fountain is ridiculous. No one uses them. Water is not hard to come by; if someone needs water that urgently it would not be a problem to find water. There was a sink with running water 10 feet away.

I even asked the inspector, "Why two fountains?"

He said it was so the standing people would not have to bend over too far. So I spent $3,000 for the two useless drinking fountains.

At the final inspection for the drinking fountains, the inspector told me that I needed tempered water in the office. He said tempered water was between 85 and 110 degrees. Another permit. I had to run an electric line to the insta hot box. Another permit. The electric lines were put in along with the insta hot, but the inspector kept rejecting the work. Of course I had to pay a fee each time they came back to re-inspect, and they would not give a time so I could meet them for the inspection.

I finally found out the reason for the rejections. I had removed all of the ceiling tiles going across the ceiling so the new electric line could be viewed by the inspector. I had not removed one tile in the corner, so the inspector was unable to see two feet of the electric line. This was the reason for the multiple rejections. There was even a ladder in the corner if the inspector felt that he really needed to take a look above the one ceiling tile.

These are some of the reasons property investors at times avoid getting permits. The cities and counties should be working with you to grow your business, but it seems they turn into your enemy and fight against you getting things done for the good of your business and the community. There are a couple communities near my residence where I would think twice about purchasing a property due to the cumbersome government interference.

Stress can rob your passion and determination to reach your goals. As we become busier and more successful, many people forget to take care of themselves. If you forget to exercise and eat properly, stress will eventually start appearing in your life. Nobody can continue to perform at his highest level if too much stress is present in his or her life.

Take the time to set a normal schedule for exercising. Your body will operate more efficiently with a normal exercise regimen.

Fail to complete

Do you have the ability to follow through on a task until completion? Most people do not. An example of this is New Year's resolutions. They usually last one or two weeks. Look back over the last couple years of your life. What goals have you made for yourself and then followed through to accomplish? I am not talking about the goal of getting five punches at the pizza shop so you can get a free pizza. I am talking about goals that positively affect your life moving forward. To be successful you have to have the attitude that you will see a goal to the end.

Most people acquire bad debt through the purchase of cars, TV's, and many other items. Bad debt ruins your financial future. Good debt plays an important part in your future plans to become wealthy. When you borrow money to earn money that is good debt. When I purchased the commercial property I mentioned earlier, I borrowed $450,000 along with my $150,000 down payment to make the purchase. This property generated an extra $30,000 in yearly revenue.

Banks are more than eager to lend money to purchase property. The physical property serves as collateral for the bank. The bank knows that if the borrower defaults on the loan they can recover the money owed to them by reselling the property. The banks are not as eager to lend money for a business. If the business fails, the banks have very little recourse to recover their money. Since the business loan is less secure, the interest rate the lender charges will be higher. The business loan generally has to be paid back in a shorter time; for example, 10 years for a business loan in comparison to 20 to 30 years for a commercial property. This shorter loan payback period means a much higher monthly loan payment.

For a new entrepreneur just starting, one may want to consider a venture with relatively low cash needed to start the business. The problem with a business loan to start the business is that right from the beginning there is pressure to make money. Falling behind on loan payments from the beginning will surely mean failure. Using the internet to start a business is a relatively low cost way to start a business. If the internet business fails, your personal finances are not ruined also.

Cash flow

I personally stopped working when my assets earned enough money so I did not have to work. As previously mentioned, my neighbor has asked me several times if I won the lottery. This neighbor could not understand how I still paid my bills but did not work at a formal job. The neighbor did not see past the idea of working to pay the bills. She and many others do not understand the power of purchasing assets to pay your bills so you do not have to work a normal job. I would rather have my assets earn me money than have to get up early each morning for work. My cash flow primarily comes from commercial property investments. My commercial properties continue to pay me day in and day out.

I have gone months without visiting a property or talking to any tenants; however, I normally visit each property every week to make sure everything is looking good. My normal process when I visit a property is to walk around the property and take pictures of any issues or maintenance work that needs to be done.

Once I get back to my office, I look back through the pictures and write down the issues on my legal pad. Each property has its own page. This is a good way to keep track of things that need to be done.

Once in a while I get bored, so I just take a drive to look at a property. Sometimes there is work to be done at a property. Finding a new tenant is what takes the most time, but that does not happen that often. If you maintain your property, tenants will stay for a long time.

Usually the work that needs to be done at a property is small in nature. Replacing sprinkler heads, a/c repair, and broken ceiling tiles are examples of common repairs. When something does need to be repaired, I rush to my phone and call the handyman or whichever contractor is right for the job. You guessed it. I do very few of the repairs myself. I decided a long time ago to focus on the things I do well, and fixing things is not one of my strong suits. Remember, you can always find somebody to pay to do any job.

Making decisions

L ife is filled with so many choices on a daily basis. There are many more psychiatrists in the
United States than in Russia. The reason is that in
the United States people have to make countless
more decisions on a daily basis, and some people
become overwhelmed. It is easier to go to your job
every day and perform the same task day in and
day out. This lifestyle is less stressful but definitely
more boring.

Being an entrepreneur requires numerous decisions on a daily basis. This is why the entrepreneur
or president of a company makes so much money.
Making many decisions can be daunting at times
even for the seasoned entrepreneur. My solution is to
gather all the information I need within two days, sit
down at the dinner table, and give myself one hour
to come up with a decision. Do not allow yourself to
become bogged down with indecisiveness. This can
paralyze you. Be aware you will not always make the
correct decision. We are human.

Recently I painted a retail property, and it looked hideous afterwards. The green color I had selected looked good sitting on my kitchen table, but on the building it was bad news. This mistake cost me $500 to repaint using a different color. The point is, as a business owner you will be faced with making many decisions. Work hard at making the best decision. Once a decision is made, move on.

After I graduated from college, I was a part-time bank teller for six months. One thing I noticed about the wealthy is that they spent their money wisely. They did not pull into the parking lot in the latest BMW, and they did not wear expensive clothing. When I saw people pull into the parking lot of the bank in a luxury vehicle, I would notice as I processed their transactions that there was not much money in their account. As the saying goes, "these people wore a big hat, but did not have any cattle". They pretended they were wealthy to "keep up with Joneses" but really were poor financially. This type of behavior eventually catches up to you and the more big hats you own, the less chance you will have of financial freedom in the future.

During the 1990s I played in a men's golf league each week, and often I would see a short guy, all dirty and with a beard, doing miscellaneous work around the golf course. His name was Al. In my mind Al was a worker doing odd jobs for the golf club, and my thought at the time was that I would say "hi" if he walked by. I had no interest in talking with him. Why would I want to waste my time? One day as I was walking up to the club to play golf, Al was digging some type of hole in the ground. I could only see him from the chest up since he was standing in the hole. I said "hi" as I walked by.

After paying my green fees in the clubhouse, I started talking with the assistant pro about how I wanted to start purchasing rental properties.

Since I had many questions at this point in my life and was not sure where to begin, the assistant pro said, "Let me introduce you to the owner. He owns this golf course and several other golf courses and has a huge portfolio of rental properties."

"OK, great!" I followed the assistant pro outside and over to the hole in the ground.

He pointed to the man standing in the hole and said, "This is Al, the owner of the club."

This person, the one to whom I did not want to give the time of day, was probably the richest man in town. He was not concerned about wearing big hats, but he had plenty of cattle. He gave me some good advice on purchasing rental properties. I almost missed out on this advice due to my preconceived notions that successful people drive expensive cars and wear fancy suits and certainly would not be found digging a ditch at a golf course.

Avoid getting attorneys involved in a property transaction and most other transactions. There are a small number of situations where the use of an attorney is worthwhile. Attorneys will end up dragging out the transaction by bringing up potential possibilities or hazards that will never happen or even if they do would not be a big deal. You will also become poor very quickly with the use of an attorney. They bill per hour, and the clock runs whether they are speaking to you or anyone else concerning your case. Just use common sense instead of an attorney.

There was a small commercial property I was interested in when I lived in Michigan. At the time I was fresh out of college and basically knew nothing about purchasing commercial properties. The realtor told me since it's a commercial property I had to hire an attorney, so I did. At the meeting between the real estate agent, attorney, and me, the attorney proclaimed we had a big problem. The attorney thought that a concrete wall at the back of the property was partially on the property we were looking to purchase and partially on someone else's property. At the time this seemed like a big issue and resulted in me not pursuing the property further.

Looking back now, I realize the concrete wall would not have been an issue. The wall had been there for at least 10 years, and no one cared whose property it was technically on. If it were to ever become an issue, someone could just remove it. It would have been cheap to remove the wall. The attorney cost me $500 and a potentially good property investment.

Play poker

When you play poker you want to give your opponents as little information as possible. You want to be as straight faced as possible so they have no idea how good a hand you have. It is many times the same in a business transaction. Do not give out unneeded information.

For example, if you are trying to purchase a mortgage company and the property it sits on for $500,000 and you believe the property alone is worth $500,000, you are not obligated to give the owner any indication of your thoughts of what the property is worth. Do not lie, be straight forward and discuss the deal as a business person, with courtesy. Nonetheless, do not let everyone know the hand you are playing.

Another example, you are trying to purchase land and you own the building next door. After purchasing you plan to expand your building. You do not have to tell the property owner that you own the building next door. This info gives the seller leverage over you.

Many times over the years real estate brokers have asked me how much cash I have to put down on a property or business that I want to purchase. The broker is calculating in his mind whether or not I actually have enough money to purchase the property or business. The broker does not want to waste his or her time. I try to answer vaguely because if they think I am light in the liquid assets (money) department they may not want to help me. Many times over the years I have been light on the money. The broker does not need to know that information, and there have been many times when I did not have enough cash to purchase an asset but still found a way to make the deal happen with creative financing or bringing in a minority partner.

10 year rule

Many people believe that it takes ten years of hard work or practice in your field to become highly successful. I believe it takes about five years of constant learning and improving with whatever you are doing to be a master at your skill. This does not mean that after five years you do not continue to learn. At the five year mark you will be knowledgeable enough to give a presentation to an auditorium of people wanting to gain knowledge of your expertise.

For example, when my wife and I started the wedding video business, we literally did not even know how to focus the camera correctly. Several years later we could explain the minute details of a video camera. We learned as the business progressed.

Attitude

Surround yourself with people who have a positive attitude. People with a bad attitude will bring you down. If you own your own business, you know that one bad apple (bad attitude) can spoil the rest. Your office and your life will become infected with negativity. People with a positive attitude will also help keep you uplifted and positive.

For example, when I was growing up every time I came up with a new business idea, which was often, my family told me very quickly that the idea was dumb, or it would not work, or you can't do that. Before long I stopped telling my family my ideas because I became tired of the negative attitude towards them. The negativity was bringing me down. What my family should have done was try to give me positive feedback along with some negative feedback. They should have told me to keep the good ideas coming.

Try your best, that's all you can do

One of the mottos I tell myself and others is to just do your best. In everyday life we all face situations of uncertainty or situations that are stressful.

Every morning I drive my daughter to school. As she is getting out the car I say, "Have a great day and do your best."

I want her to know that doing her best is more important to me than getting a letter grade of A or B. I also know that someone who consistently does his best, whether it is at school, on the job, or in a new business, is the type of person who will be successful.

If I am consistently trying my best, I am moving myself, my family, and my business in the right direction. I also try to improve on things on a daily, weekly, or yearly basis. The properties I own and manage are a good example. They are in constant need of repairs. My thoughts are not only to keep them managed and maintained well, but to slowly, over time, continue to improve each property. This may entail such things as improving the landscaping, painting, or just picking up some trash in back. It is not a coincidence or luck that my properties stay 100% occupied.

Get a good deal/asset value

The value of a property or business is mostly determined by your experience and doing a thorough investigation. Many real estate investors look primarily at the income the property generates. In my opinion that is a small part of the story on why or why not a particular property would be a good investment.

Some examples: Let's say the property is bringing in a good cash flow relative to price, but a hair salon rents 75% of the total space and is paying rents that are 50% above the going rate in the area because the current owner of the building owns the salon (he is paying himself). Also, the hair salon may go out of business or close if the owner wants to retire. So I would not look favorably on this investment due to the future outlook even though the current numbers look good.

The other end of the spectrum is a property with poor cash flow relative to price. On paper this may look like a terrible deal. This property is currently 60% vacant, and the tenants who are leasing space pay 50% less than the current market rents. However, this property is on a main road in a growing part of town. This is the type of property I look for. The future potential for this type of property is excellent. The value of the property can be increased very quickly over a short period of time. Once the value is increased, you can refinance to pull money out of the property. This money is tax free. The property was not sold so it is not a taxable event. Then what? You guessed it. This money will be used for the next property investment.

Sometimes it can be difficult to finance these types of properties because the bank loans money on cash flow. I try to show them the future potential of the property. When the bank is reluctant to finance a property due to poor cash flow relative to price, you will most likely have to put more cash down to do the deal. If you have no more cash, you may have to bring in a minority partner. Make sure the partner is a minority partner so you maintain control of the business. You keep control by having a least 51% ownership.

Once you gain experience and have a track record that you **pay your bills on time, all the time,** the lender will start becoming more flexible on the terms of the loan and ultimately help you get more deals done faster.

This is where you turn into a detective. Gather all the information you can get your hands on about the property to make the most informed decision you can.

I had a friend a few years back who was looking to purchase an office building that would be good for two tenants. He had already negotiated a price with the seller and was working with a contractor to renovate the property. This was during his due diligence period. My friend knew I purchased and sold commercial property so he asked me to stop by to give him my assessment. The property was in poor condition, inside and out, but that was not what I was concerned about. I told my friend to come out to the parking lot with me and to look around.

I then asked him, "What do you see?"

He looked around, and said, "Wow."

What he was looking at was a run down, dead part of town. There were no cars driving by. There were some neglected and vacant houses and two empty lots for sale next door.

I said, "Would you want to rent space here to run your business?"

He said, "Probably not."

I asked if he had called the realtors regarding the two vacant lots that were for sale. When he said no, I told him I had called from my car a few minutes ago. The lots had been for sale for three years, and the realtor told me to make any offer if I was interested. This part of town was older, dilapidated, depressed, and not improving anytime soon.

I told my friend that I hoped he was not upset with my comments. He had asked for my opinion, and I thought it was only fair that I give it to him free of sugar coating. I said if this area was in the path of new development, even if ten years down the road, or if on a major road in at least an average part of town, I would say go for it. My friend had fallen in love with this property. Big mistake. After being shocked by my comments, he eventually cancelled the contract and did not purchase the property.

Listening (so you will not get ripped off in the future)

Becoming more knowledgeable and understanding how something works or learning about new changes in your business is accomplished primarily through listening.

Recently I had to call the septic company because the distribution box collapsed, and sewage was running out into the back of the property. The point here is that I made sure to listen in order to learn as much as possible about septic systems and try to make sure I was not being ripped off. The quote for repair was $1950.00. Shocking. Fortunately for me, I have worked with this septic company for a while and through my past experience of listening to septic contractors, I knew this was a fair deal.

I have a black book of contact info that lists recommended contractors for just about any job that needs to be done. I also have a list of contractors to stay away from. I write notes under each contractor to explain why I should or should not work with this company in the future. I am basically writing myself a note for the future.

We all have issues. That is not a good enough reason!

Everyone has excuses for why they do not want to do something. I am too busy, I have a cold, now is not a good time, I am too tired, I hurt my shoulder playing tennis, we are going on vacation, and so many more excuses I could write a book about it.

The fact is everyone is living life with the many challenges and issues that life presents. If we wait for that perfect time when the stars are aligned, we will not take action. There will always be reasons why you should not pursue your dreams. The successful person just pushes forward and makes it happen. To the successful person, it does not matter if he has a cold, hurt his shoulder, is tired, or is planning a vacation. We are only alive about 25,000 days on average, so you should make the most of your life.

I have heard the phrase, "I am judgment proof right now" several times lately. Basically, what this means is that I have no money and I will not be sued because I have no money. It is better not to be judgment proof. That means you have some level of wealth. Many lawyer friends of mine are afraid of lawsuits, which is understandable because of their field of work. There are no guarantees against a lawsuit, but being afraid of a lawsuit is no way to live your life.

Lawsuits are minimized by doing things correctly: setting up LLC's or incorporating, proper liability insurance, maintaining properties, and using sound practices in the operation of a business.

I have had one lawsuit at my commercial properties over the last eight years. The tenant wanted me to replace four a/c systems even though three separate companies said they were operating correctly. We went to mediation and could not come to an agreement. After the mediation I decided to replace the four a/c units thinking this would end the lawsuit. This did **not** end the lawsuit. The tenant wanted me to pay $15,000 in legal fees that he had accumulated. My attorney said I would probably win the lawsuit in court, but I would probably end up paying my attorney $20,000 in legal fees to save $15,000. Even though I would most likely prevail in court, I paid the $15,000 in legal fees to be done with the lawsuit.

It is important to stay on top of situations and to find resolutions even if you did nothing wrong or the problem does not involve you.

Take charge and be determined

I know many people who are content in their everyday 9-5 jobs, or at least they tell me that. One good example is a friend of mine who states things are going well at the job he has had for the last 10 years. He drives old cars and is always concerned about money and what things cost. Maybe he is happy in that lifestyle, but I know I would not be. I do not want to be forced to go into the office every day, and besides I like to sleep in. I would rather drive a Porsche than a 7-year-old Toyota Camry.

Many people have good ideas and good intentions of starting businesses. However, many people lack the ability to take a risk so they are doomed to remain in their jobs. Successful people have the ability to take calculated risks. A calculated risk is weighing the risks and benefits of a deal and deciding that the benefits outweigh the risks. Many people get to this point and decide that the benefits outweigh the risks, but then get scared or worry about some minor issue and do not move forward with the deal.

In the 1990's I was involved with a partner, a doctor, to purchase a golf course. We had agreed on the sale price, looked at the financials, inspected the course, and after moving through the process for over three months were ready to sign the agreement and move forward. The day before signing the agreement, my partner called and said he would like to take one more look at the property before going forward. While we were taking another look everything seemed to be in order, and in my mind it was confirming we had a good deal in purchasing this golf course.

As we were driving back to the club house in our golf carts, my partner noticed a rusted sprinkler head and questioned why this was rusted.

"They have probably been using these sprinkler heads for a long time," I said. "Even though this one is rusted, it is still working fine. If that is something that bothers you, it is only a $20 item to replace."

For the rest of the day and that evening all I heard my partner talk about was rusted sprinkler heads. I knew right then he was looking for a way to get out of the deal without just flat changing his mind and making himself look bad. Sure enough, the next morning he called to tell me that based on the sprinkler heads he felt we would uncover more run down equipment and problems with the golf course so he did not want to move forward. I said, no problem. What else could I say? There was no point in getting into an argument about it.

This is a good example of the golf course being a good buy, but since my partner became nervous about making the deal nothing happened. I would have personally moved forward with the deal; however, at the time my partner was contributing 60% of the down payment, and I could not make the purchase on my own.

Risk is often associated with something bad. To me the word corresponds more closely to courage and strength. I am obviously not talking about the risk of betting on a horse at the track. When you have done your homework on a business you want to start (or property you want to purchase) and you know in the back of your mind it will be successful, you need to push forward and make it happen.

Setting up your business is the easiest part of starting a business. It is also one of the most important things to do. If you operate your business as a sole proprietor or partnership, you put all of your personal assets at financial risk. For example, John Smith goes into business selling socks and sets up the business as John Smith dba Sock World. (DBA stands for Doing Business As). A person wearing one of Sock World's socks slips on her kitchen floor breaking her neck. The injured person can sue not only Sock World; she can also sue John Smith. John Smith has now placed all of his assets in jeopardy.

Since people tend to file lawsuits more frequently in today's world, protect your personal assets. The simplest way to protect your personal assets is to set up an LLC (Limited Liability Company) or Type S Corporation. These business structures protect your personal assets from lawsuit. The annual tax returns can be put through your normal personal tax returns. This makes the tax preparation process fairly simple. Talk to an accountant to determine which business entity is the best fit for your particular business.

Some attorneys claim they can pierce through an LLC and get to your personal assets if there is a lawsuit. If your business is operated correctly I do not believe that piercing through the LLC can easily be done (my opinion). To prevent the small possibility of an attorney trying to get to your personal assets, if possible, setup a two member LLC.

The LLC was created so businesses would not risk their personal assets with a business venture, but still allows for the ease of reporting income on your personal tax return.

Setting up an LLC or corporation is uncomplicated. The hardest part is picking out the name. The name you choose must end with LLC if it is a Limited Liability Company. The LLC can be set up over the phone by calling the I.R.S. @ 800-829-4933 or by going online @ www.irs.gov. It literally takes about 10 minutes. Once completed you will have your Federal ID and will be able to operate your new business as an LLC or corporation.

Many states also require you to register your new business. In my state of Florida, this can be done very easily online @ Sunbiz.org. Please do not pay an attorney or CPA to set up your LLC; it is too easy to not do on your own. I paid an attorney $500 to set up my first LLC. What a waste of money. If you plan on having employees, you may want to incorporate under a subchapter S.

Legalzoom.com is an inexpensive online company that can help those that do not want to setup the business by themselves.

Set up business checking accounts, and do not use personal accounts for business affairs. If this is a home business, I would recommend purchasing a PO Box at the local post office. I would also set up a separate phone number for business calls only. I currently use Ooma. The point is to operate your business as a business and not mix personal matters.

To conclude

Your passion is everything. Do what you love and love what you do. Whatever your passion, if you do it better than anyone else you will be rich. I know a person who is passionate about making nuts and bolts. His business has grown very large, and he is quite successful. When I talk with him he talks about nuts and bolts, and I can hear the passion in his voice.

Listen to your inner passion. Believe in yourself because you can do it. I want to encourage you in your business ventures by sharing some of the things I have learned.

Good luck on your future endeavors. **Now get up and do it**.

Make it Happen

Passion + Determination

plus

Business + Real Estate

=

Wealth